God, in speaking through the prophets Haggai and Zechariah, called his people to examine their reality and return to him. In a very real sense, Conrad Kanagy has the spirit of the prophets in asking the church to recognize our own reality and return to the God who has called us. By coming to grips with the truth of where we are, our roadblocks to returning are being torn down as God is dismantling the church as it is, in order to build his kingdom.

-Rick Noyes, Fruit Heights, Utah

In 2020 and thereafter, in the midst of the toxic mix of a global pandemic and national politics, in a society full of rampant anxiety and fear, and the shaking apart of many things, there stands the church that is also shaking and crumbling in the process of being dismantled. Some of us are listening for a voice to help us understand what is God up to. God has used Conrad Kanagy's voice to bring insight and clarity to our ongoing journey of faith, for which I am most grateful. Will the western Church rise up to become more than a stagnant institution? Or will it decay into a relic of the past? Read on, for this book will be well worth your time.

-Dale Good, Lancaster, PA

I have more than a passing interest in this project, having listened to a number of Dr. Kanagy's podcasts. I find them compassionate, learned, and thought provoking. To my mind they represent a shared ideal in the fi   f academic scholarship and faith-based leadership—a braci   nest search to identify the reas   viduals and communities, livin   moment.

*   bethtown, PA*

This project is quite ambitious. It began as an inquiry into the disruption of social life and social institutions resulting from the pandemic of 2020. It evolved into an integrated set of essays offering an exposition of: (1) the effect of increasing institutionalization and modernization of the church with respect to matters of faith, (2) the influence of religion upon society, (3) the influence of society upon religion, and (4) how a disruption in what we take for granted can provide a reorientation of our lives and our faith. The methodology for this undertaking is comprised of an integration of theology and sociology. Mission accomplished.

-Mike Schwartz, Elizabethtown, PA

A Church Dismantled asks more questions than it answers, and that is what makes it special. In an era of toxic "certainty" that divides and destroys, Conrad Kanagy invites us to lean into the uncertainty of this pandemic era, and to question everything we thought we knew about what the church should be, what Jesus would have us do, and what it means to love our neighbor. This collection of prophetic essays, derived from Dr. Kanagy's podcast, "A Church Dismantled—A Kingdom Restored," has at its core the earth-shaking revelation that God may have been using the COVID-19 pandemic to summon us to "being the Church" rather than simply "going to church," which is what God has intended for us all along.

-Sarah Santos, Minneapolis, MN

A CHURCH
DISMANTLED
A KINGDOM RESTORED

*Why Is God Taking
Apart the Church?*

CONRAD L. KANAGY

A CHURCH DISMANTLED—A KINGDOM RESTORED
Why Is God Taking Apart the Church?

Copyright © 2021

All rights reserved.

Scripture quotations unless noted otherwise are from *The New Oxford Annotated Bible,* copyright © 1991, Oxford University Press, Inc.; *New Revised Standard Version of the Bible* (NRSV), copyright © 1989, Division of Christian Education of the National Council of the Churches of Christ in the United States of America. Used by permission. All rights reserved.

Scripture quotations noted KJV are from The Authorized (King James) Version. Rights in the Authorized Version in the United Kingdom are vested in the Crown. Reproduced by permission of the Crown's patentee, Cambridge University Press.

Six lines of lyrics from Wayne Watson's song, "Home Free," reprinted with the author's permission.

Selection from Henk Stenvers, "Walking on Water," Part 1, "Concerning the Future of the Dutch Mennonites" (Algemene Doopsgezinde Societëit), Feb. 3, 2021, reprinted with the author's permission.

Two lines from Sydney Carter's "Lord of the Dance" (1963) reprinted with permission of Stainer & Bell (U.K.)

Library of Congress Control Number: 2021945085
International Standard Book Number: 978-1-60126-755-9

Masthof Press
219 Mill Road | Morgantown, PA 19543-9516
www.Masthof.com

MORE BY CONRAD L. KANAGY

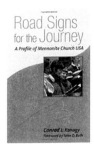

Road Signs for the Journey:
A Profile of Mennonite Church USA
(Harrisonburg, VA: Herald Press, 2007)

Road Signs for the Journey: A Study of Denominational Decline--and
the Discovery of Hope in the Spirit's Dismantling of the Church
by Amazon.com Services LLC
Learn more: https://www.amazon.com/dp/B09C1PTFRP/ref=cm_
sw_em_r_mt_dp_JVQAB6TYYSTXQJAPTZGT

CO-AUTHORED BY CONRAD L. KANAGY

Winds of the Spirit: A Profile of Anabaptist Churches in the Global
South by Amazon.com
Learn more: https://www.amazon.com/dp/0836196368/ref=cm_
sw_em_r_mt_dp_E1A3N248FJ6WMN4Z038V

The Riddles of Human Society, Conrad L. Kanagy and Donald B.
Kraybill (CA: SAGE Publications, 1999)

TO HEIDI

God knew that I needed a life-long partner,
who when I finally showed up as my most authentic self,
would already be there waiting for me.

"No churches to encircle God
And pen him up—a common fugitive"

—*Reynolds Price, "All Will Be Whole" (after Rilke)*

TABLE OF CONTENTS

FOREWORD

Wherever you look, the metrics for the institutional church spell doom. A recent headline from the Pew Research Center proclaims, "In U.S., Decline of Christianity Continues at Rapid Pace."[1] Fewer people identify as practicing Christians; more and more say they are atheists, agnostics, "nones," or spiritual but not religious. Other indicators of religious commitment are also slipping. Generation Z—the cohort born from 1997 to 2015 and nurtured on all things digital—has been dubbed "the first post-Christian generation." Even though the long-term effects of the Covid shutdown remain uncertain, the future of Christianity in America appears gloomy.

Amid this dire forecast for the institutional church, Conrad Kanagy offers a vision of hope and dispels gloom. He sees the hand of God enabling what he calls the dismantling of the church. And why would God be doing such a shocking thing? To prepare the way, to restore the kingdom first described by the prophet Isaiah and later echoed by John the Baptist who paved the way for the kingdom announced by Jesus. And if God's Spirit is directing this grand dismantling of the church as we know it, then Christian leaders, says Kanagy, should align themselves with the project, not try to obstruct it.

Dismantling involves taking something apart piece by piece. In the fashion world, a mantle is a sleeveless cloth, a cloak, shawl, or stole that covers the body. Dismantling the institutional church

---

[1] https://www.pewforum.org/2019/10/17/in-u-s-decline-of-christianity-continues-at-rapid-pace/.

involves unwrapping layer upon layer of mantles that hide the body. God is dismantling these socially constructed mantles that have accumulated over the generations—dense theologies, religious falsehoods, erroneous myths, centralized power, religious red tape, and ritualized formulas for proper worship, all of which obscure the body, meaning the original core of Christian faith and practice.

For Kanagy, the decline of the church is ironically the handiwork of God's dismantling of the institutionalized church as we know it. This process of dismantling, he suggests, reveals the real core of Christian faith: Jesus. Inspired by the vision of three Hebrew prophets—Isaiah, Jeremiah, and Jesus—Kanagy reminds us that things are not always what they appear to be. Where others see catastrophe, he sees God's handiwork. Where others see disaster, he sees God's Spirit at work.

The Hebrew prophets unveiled the myths, the lies, and the idolatry of God's wayward people. Conrad Kanagy shows us how the message of the Hebrew prophets helps us interpret and make sense out of the sweeping changes in church life today. Instead of decrying the unraveling of the established church, he invites us to see the changes through God's eyes and to join in the work of the Holy Spirit. When religious professionals try to fix the broken church, Kanagy summons us not to repair it, but, like Isaiah of old, to prepare for God's coming kingdom.

It may sound audacious to say that God is dismantling the church, but that's exactly what Jesus, *God incarnate,* was doing during his ministry. He dismantled many of the entrenched practices and traditions of his time. Prophets are disruptors. They shake up the status quo. Jesus shook up the keepers and defenders of institutional religion. His scathing criticism condemned the Pharisees and Sadducees for developing religious regulations galore that placed heavy burdens on the poor.

In a flagrant violation of the rules that forbade "work" on the Sabbath, he healed the sick and shelled grain for the poor. And he sought to shut down the mighty Jerusalem temple by flipping the tables of the money changers who had turned it into a lucrative market to rip off poor peasants who came to offer their sacrifices—the only institutionalized pathway to forgiveness. Dozens of his parables critiqued the callous attitudes of religious leaders. Jesus described the pious powerbrokers as filthy cups on the inside that looked clean on the outside, and as polished tombs that stank on the inside. Finally, he scorned the sham piety of leaders who touted their righteousness when their hearts were filled with hypocrisy and lawlessness. In all of these ways Jesus dismantled the pillars and practices of institutional religion that perverted true faith and worship of Almighty God.

More importantly, Jesus announced God's new upside-down kingdom that showcased God's relentless, unconditional love. The new kingdom welcomed outsiders, nobodies, and the stigmatized. It welcomed the demoniacs, the lepers, the blind, the deaf, the lame, the ill, and the paralyzed as well as prostitutes, tax collectors, sinners, adulterers, widows, Samaritans, women, and Gentiles. In short, Jesus hung out with a big band of nobodies from nowhere. He welcomed the throwaways tossed on the social trash pile. Instead of spitting on them, he touched them, loved them, and named them God's people.

When captured and tortured and placed on trial, Jesus demonstrated God's nonviolent love in the face of terror. Love is the bright marquee message in Kanagy's essays. He shows how God's love has no boundaries or favorites.

About four years ago, Kanagy learned that he had Parkinson's disease. This difficult but liberating experience brought a personal dismantling that transformed his life. Among other things, it prompted a blitz of 275 episodes in a year-long podcast with 50,000 downloads in eighty countries. The thirty-eight essays in this book originate from the podcast that began in May 2020.

The Parkinson's dismantling gave Kanagy the courage, the guts, and the grit to strip off his masks and speak the truth. It empowered him to say and write things that most of us might think but would never say. Setting aside his inhibitions freed him to reveal his innermost thoughts and struggles.

These essays mingle the voice of a prophet, the eye of a sociologist, the heart of a pastor, the wisdom of an educator, and, above all, the candid confessions of a child of God. Whatever your identities—religious, skeptic, political, racial, gender, class—you will find his essays provocative. His unvarnished honesty and his picturesque language are refreshing. Kanagy invites us to see things in new ways that jolt our spiritual complacency.

You may not agree with him on every point, but you will admire his courage to say it as he sees it. He may stir your ire or light your fire, annoy you or compel you to compassion. Prophetic voices do that. But you will keep on reading. His poignant stories, evocative phrases, and frank confessions will entice you to read on and on to the very last line. I promise!

—Donald B. Kraybill, author of *The Upside-Down Kingdom*, 1978, revised edition 2018.

ACKNOWLEDGMENTS

This book, written over the past year, is the first of what I anticipate to be a book series entitled "A Church Dismantled—A Kingdom Restored," based upon podcast themes about which I wrote during the pandemic: a church dismantled, ministry in a dismantled church, light and darkness in a church dismantled, and my own journey through a dismantled church. The current book is organized thematically, reflecting some of those themes. To provide a contextual timeframe, each chapter indicates the month in which it was written.

I have so many persons to acknowledge and thank for their support of this project over the past year and longer. I have walked with my wife Heidi for more than three decades, and she more than anyone has influenced my love for God's Word and the truths found in the holy scripture. I have been deeply formed by her and by our journey together. She has supported this project and all of the endeavors to which God has called me over the decades. Their value has increased greatly for having emerged as they have "out of our marriage."

For years, Heidi asked me whether my sermons spoke to everyone who showed up for the Sunday service. While for a time I resisted the question, I came to appreciate it deeply because it challenged me to abandon my scholarly jargon and ivory tower pretense, and to speak in language and story that could communicate to everyone—from children to the elderly and to those with little education as well as those with much. After all, it is "to infants" that such things are revealed, as Jesus said, unlike to "the wise and the intelligent" (Luke 10:21).

For this reason I asked some of my most consistent listeners to offer their reflections on the book, not because they are scholars or theologians necessarily, but because they are ordinary folks who also hear God's voice and have heard that voice within the words of the podcast upon which this book is based. Their encouragement over the past year has motivated me to keep on writing and sharing what I sensed God was giving me to speak. They have helped me to remember that I am not as alone as I often think I am when feeling without a theological or ecclesiastical home these days.

I am especially grateful to my friend of nearly two decades— Mike "the Bike Guy" Schwartz—for numerous conversations across the years that have sharpened my sensitivity to what God is doing in the world. Despite the fact that we do not share the same religious commitments, or perhaps because of that fact, Mike's personal and sociological perspective has been invaluable to me.

Elizabethtown College for nearly three decades has given me space to engage in my church related research and practice of ministry. Across four college administrations I have been blessed by the same support and encouragement, without which I would not have been able to "pastor" as a minister and "profess" as a teacher at the same time. In keeping with what I have always experienced, the college has supported and promoted the podcast "A Church Dismantled—A Kingdom Restored" and has publicized my efforts widely. The college has also given me a sabbatical for the fall of 2021 to continue to write and publish my work.

Our congregation at Elizabethtown Mennonite Church has graciously been a space for me over the last decade to hone my preaching and writing for an audience that lives and labors in the everyday world of work, home, and play.

I wish to thank my editor, Charles Davidson, for the amazing way that he has walked with me, encouraged me from the very moment he set eyes on the manuscript, has helped to broaden and deepen my writing, and has believed in this project from the beginning of our work together. I want to thank the readers of the various drafts of the manuscript, including Sarah Santos and Paul Roth who listened closely for the continuation and consistency of my message and my voice as Charles and I worked through several iterations of the manuscript. Charles gave the confidence to me that I needed to launch this project and was just the editor I needed to do so. I will be forever grateful.

I am both humbled and honored by Walter Brueggemann's willingness to write the major endorsement for this book. I relied heavily upon Walter's work in the writing of *Road Signs for the Journey* in 2006-7. To have him endorse the current project in which my prophetic voice was reawakened once again, fifteen years later, is indeed a gift of God's Spirit.

Dan Mast of Masthof Press has been a valued collaborator on this project and has postured himself to do whatever possible to speed this book along, to keep the pricing reasonable, and to add helpful counsel along the way.

I also want to thank the members of my Facebook group "A Church Dismantled" and to the Book Launch Team for their ambitious collaboration and their ongoing support. They have been a consistent source of affirmation and have helped me to feel less homeless and less alone in this dismantled church.

Thanks go to publicist Rob Eagar for his excellent counsel and direction in thinking about how to market this book and those that follow.

Finally, I am grateful for the willingness of my long-time mentor, friend, and colleague, Professor Donald B. Kraybill of Elizabethtown College, for writing the foreword to this book and for recognizing a kinship in it to his own now-classic title, *An Upside-Down Kingdom* (Herald Press, 1978). From the earliest days of my career to the present, and across hundreds of hours of collaboration, Don has poured wisdom into my life—always honest, always gentle, always gracious. As Mike the Bike Guy says about Don, "You just always feel better about yourself after hanging out with him!"

All of these essays were written during the Covid pandemic.[2] I have sought to retain, for the most part, the present tense in which they were originally penned. This book and the podcast episodes that preceded it represent for me the intersection and integration of various areas of my professional and personal life that had been disparate entities in the past. They have allowed me to draw upon nearly three decades of teaching sociology, thirty-five years of sociological research, fifteen years of church and denominational consulting, twenty years of pastoral ministry, my childhood and coming-of-age in a conservative Mennonite-Amish community, my life-long struggle with a terror of God's wrath exacerbated by obsessive-compulsive disorder, and the diagnosis, four years ago, of Parkinson's disease.

As you will read throughout the chapters of this book, the Parkinson's diagnosis has been a difficult but transformative experience for me, and in an uncanny way has represented my own dismantling at the same time that I have been writing about the dismantling of the church. But as you will hear me say repeatedly, this disease has given me a timeline and horizon that I had not seen so clearly before, and it has brought with it an encounter with the love of God, a re-conversion to Jesus, and an outpouring of his Spirit in ways I had not previously experienced in my life, which has led to freedom, clarity of identity, and a sense of contentment like unto none I had known before. As I have often said, if it finally took Parkinson's disease to

---

2   Hereafter cited as "Covid."

bring these gifts to me, then thanks be to God! For it may just be that these graces also ensure that I find my way, finally, "home."

My prayer is that my reflections throughout this book and the future volumes, *To Tear Down or Build Up? Ministry in a Church Dismantled*; *The Light Still Shines: Discovering Good News in a Church Dismantled*; and *My Story, My Song: A Dismantled Life Within a Church Dismantled*, will be an encouragement to you, and will cast a bit of light on your own journey toward the new heaven and new earth that is just over the horizon.

So, accompanied by the gracious words of the apostle Paul, himself plagued by weakness and troubled with a thorn in the flesh that God would not remove, may you receive my words, like Paul's, as means of encouragement. For, in the midst of the dismantling: "We do not lose heart. Even though our outer nature is wasting away, our inner nature is being renewed day by day. For this slight momentary affliction is preparing us for an eternal weight of glory beyond all measure, because we look not at what can be seen but at what cannot be seen; for what can be seen is temporary, but what cannot be seen is eternal" (2 Cor 4:16-18).

—Conrad L. Kanagy, Elizabethtown, PA
June 28, 2021

READERS' RESOURCES:
The website www.achurchdismantled.com
contains resources to support the material in
this book, including a short video in which I
address each of the seven sections of the book
as well as study guides for personal or group
reflection and discussion. Readers may contact me directly through the website.

PART ONE

A LIFE DISMANTLED—
A LIFE RESTORED

CHAPTER ONE

From Pandemic to Podcast

In May of 2020, during the early months of the Covid pandemic, I wrote what I simply call the "Weekly Email" to our congregation, where my wife Heidi and I have served as a ministry couple for fifteen years. I entitled that week's message "Why the Church Cannot Be Re-opened," which was my reaction to the incessant calls of local church leaders to "get back to church" as soon as possible.

That little piece caught the attention of a few folks who then passed it on to others, which led to a series of blog-like postings on Facebook and eventually to a year-long podcast of 275 episodes. The primary theme of the podcast was at least fifteen years in the making, and was based upon research on the American church that I conducted in 2006–7, resulting in a book entitled *Road Signs for the Journey*.[3]

At that time, I raised the question: "Is God's Spirit dismantling the church because we have so failed God's mission?" For me the question has now become rhetorical, since I do embrace the idea that God is up to a grand deconstruction or dismantling—a taking apart—of the church as we know it and as it has been constructed in the West. This question was quickly followed by another: "If this is what God's Spirit is doing, then how can we as leaders work with the Spirit rather than against the Spirit?"

At the onset of the Covid pandemic, I quickly saw this moment as a season that was rich with transformational opportuni-

---

[3] Conrad Kanagy, *Road Signs for the Journey: A Profile for Mennonite Church USA* (Harrisonburg, VA: Herald Press, 2007).

ties for the church, if only we would see and embrace them. For over the past century the church in the West has staked its future on the rational structures of modernity—on Enlightenment ideals about what is real and true and right and good. But little have we understood just how vulnerable we have made ourselves by doing so. It's almost as if some days we have thrown Jesus in as an afterthought.

Over the years, I have repeatedly cautioned my students that we have no idea whether modernity is sustainable or not. When we embrace the cultures and structures of modernity, we are vulnerable to whatever attacks them. Given our confidence in the reliability of empiricism and science, the last thing we expected was a virus from the Dark Ages to threaten the modern foundations upon which we have built the church. My concern at the onset of Covid was that if we fail to be honest about how thoroughly accommodated the church has become to modernity, including its economic and political manifestations, then we would unlikely be able to weather the pain and discomfort of the Spirit's reorientation of the church during the pandemic. I repeatedly stated, "If we are not converted to the ways of Jesus in this moment, we may never be."

Yet, as the months rolled along, I began to sense frustration among some of the saints who wondered, "Conrad, just what do you mean by the dismantling of the church, and how long will you keep rattling the same cage?"

I responded along these lines: I believe the Spirit is deconstructing, or tearing down, or taking apart the socially constructed elements of the church that recently have become—or for a long time have been—irrelevant to the central message of the gospel. That is to say, ways of being the church that have lost sight of the essential meaning and purpose of the church, ways of interpreting scripture that have justified remaining culture-bound and period-bound, and

In what way has Church Compromised Gospel? One
Main way is by Embracing materialist

ways of forming political alliances with the principalities and powers
that have terribly compromised the message of Jesus. *Rationalism*

This deconstruction may require eliminating tiresome com-
mittee meetings spent more on decisions about who will clean the
church than about who will care for the diversity of neighbors in
all degrees of circumstances surrounding the church—and spent on
anything else that takes our eyes off of the imperatives of the gospel
to which Jesus urgently summons us in mission.

Parenthetically, our youth flee the church, not as pagans who
renounce the church, but as insightful persons who may see more
clearly than the rest of us just what the church has become.

For me, dismantling the church is about joining God's grand
excavation project of Isaiah 40, which has captured my imagination
ever since I was a child, by lowering mountains that are barriers to
the shalom of God's coming kingdom, by raising valleys in which the
marginalized have had to hide for fear of being overrun by those who
hold the power strings, and by making crooked paths straight and
rough places a level plain along which the lost, the wounded, and the
destitute may find their way home. Contrary to the vision of Isaiah,
the church too often has done the opposite, by erecting mountains,
deepening valleys, and making pathways rougher and more crooked
than they already were.

Some have noted that I sound a bit angry at times as I write.
Or they feel condemned by my writing. Yes, sometimes I do feel
angry—angry that the church has built edifices and theologies and
policies in keeping with the prevailing materialistic, mechanistic,
and rationalistic ethos of modernity that the larger society takes for
granted, but which has cast a long shadow over the good news of the
freedom, joy, love, kindness, grace, and, yes, judgment, that God revealed in Jesus Christ. For it is not to the ethos of modernity that we
are called to be obedient, and by which we are to be judged as faith-

ful, but rather in obedience to and by the transcendent judgment of him whose name we bear as Christians.

Which brings me to the second aspect of what I mean by the Spirit's dismantling of the church, and that is the removal of those "mantles" of our own devising that we have placed on the church and the Christian faith, which cover up the truths of God's kingdom that we are called to live by as our truths. The dismantling that I identify in this book has been both personal and autobiographical, as I confess my own false mantles while calling out the false mantles of the church that have displaced the true mantle of Christ—whether those false mantles be imposed upon any one or all of us, or upon God, or upon the Church itself.[4]

From very early on as a child, I was caught in cycles of torment and depression characteristic of obsessive-compulsiveness, which were fed by the oppressiveness of an "old order" of cultural fog that emphasized goodness, performance, perfection, and then, on top of it all, God's wrath. So whenever I failed to hit the high mark, which was every moment of every day, I remember these kinds of thoughts: Am I the only sinner among this bunch of saints? Are all the others okay with their sins? Do they know some secret about how to survive with a guilty conscience, which no one has shared with me? And finally, I don't understand why everyone says the gospel is so wonderful, when to me, given the way it's laid on like a razor strop applied to one's tender behind, it feels like hell instead of good news.

Slowly and over time, I began to understand that what the church had done (and all too often still does) was to "mantle" (as in "muzzle") the truth, by declaring one thing while being altogether

---

4   When I reference the Church with a capital "C," I am referring to the Church eternal and universal. References to the church and churches with a lower case "c" reflect those institutions of our own construction as well as the local embodiment of the Church universal.

PART ONE: *A Life Dismantled—a Life Restored*

comfortable with something else, that is, by marketing its "product" with false advertising and claiming that the naked emperor wore a fine suit of clothes and his wife a starched bonnet, when what I saw underneath was something altogether different.

To mantle means to cover up and smooth over. And, dear folks, you and I both know that the church has too often covered up truths and smoothed over falsehoods. This is why I recently reacted so strongly to an invitation to speak to a group of churches for whom the stated aim of the weekend was to reinforce their desire to separate themselves from the world, as a way of feeling reassured about their goodness in contrast to the darkness of the world. I reacted because I detected that old shibboleth, that better-than-everybody-else-separatism. At the same time, I knew too much about some of the congregations within this group of churches in order to feel comfortable "remantling" their pretense to an unworldliness and other-worldliness that needs to be dismantled.

It was recognizing the false mantles of the church for what they are that saved me from giving up on God. And I suspect that I will spend the rest of my days doing the work of dismantling if it means that even one more person could be set free, as I have been set free over the course of this past year—set free by the One named Jesus who so dismantled the religious arrogance and edifices of his day that it cost him his life in order to save the world.

In 2017, I was diagnosed with Parkinson's Disease at the age of 52 years. For the first year, I cried and raged as I grieved the losses to come. But over time, I have also begun to recognize the gifts that I am receiving as a result of this disease. One of those gifts is the clarity with which I now see the horizon ahead, and the knowledge that my days of quality health are limited. This recognition has been transformative for me, as I realize that my own body is being dismantled at the same time that the church itself is being dismantled.

My weaknesses are being exposed, and the mantles I wore to cover those weaknesses have been stripped away. I can't hide my vulnerabilities or deny my fragility. Over the past four years I have had a new conversion to Jesus and a new awareness of God's incredible love for his children—meaning every and all human beings created with the imprint of God upon them. I have little doubt that the podcast or this book would ever have emerged without this disease taking me by surprise, but which I now realize to be my own unique path Home.

It has been clear to me during the past year that I am not alone in my sense that the church is in the process of being dismantled. The podcast "A Church Dismantled—A Kingdom Restored" has appealed to many more listeners than I ever imagined it would. Nearly 50,000 episodes have been downloaded in more than 80 countries and nearly 1,600 cities. My writing has had a special appeal, it seems, to folks who have become disillusioned with the American church and have perhaps left that church. I call these folks the diaspora—those who have left what we have long presumed to be the primary institution by which one discovers the kingdom of God but which too often is the one that leads folks in the wrong direction or in no direction at all.

Do I still believe in the Church? Yes. I believe that the one who founded the Church (upper case) is also the one who is now taking apart much of what we have constructed of the church (lower case) that fails to be the people that Jesus calls to be the light and the salt of the earth.

I believe in Jesus. And I remain committed to the Church eternal and universal and to the church that is temporal and local, composed of divinely inspired communities encountering and living fully within the mystery of a loving, compassionate, and caring God who made himself vulnerable to us by entering our world through the embodiment of his Son.

My continued discovery of the Holy One means that I must join his Spirit in the grand excavation project envisioned in Isaiah 40, which the Spirit initiated—for lowering mountains, raising valleys, and making rough places smooth and crooked places straight!

CHAPTER TWO

"This Is My Story and This Is My Song," and Why It Took 55 Years for Me to Sing It

July 2020

Following my sermon one Sunday, which was focused on my grief over the losses that I and so many of us had suffered during this pandemic, I was approached by one of the saints who was concerned about what he had heard in my podcast.

Taken by surprise, I hemmed and hawed from behind my mask. I was tired from having preached, especially since my message was filled with lament. I stuttered a few things about the podcast, trying to explain to him where I was coming from. And I'm sure I came across as a bit defensive.

As I turned away, the answer that I wish I had given him suddenly came to me from the titles to two old hymns I love: "Just as I Am, Without One Plea" and "Blessed Assurance . . . This Is My Story, This Is My Song." Accordingly, I thought, he may not agree with "my story and my song," and he may not appreciate me "just as I am," but nevertheless "this is my story" and "this is my song." And I shall tell it and sing it forever in the presence of the One who receives me "just as I am."

There are so many reasons why I have hesitated over the years to tell my story and sing my song, but mainly because I feared the reaction of some of the saints. You know, don't you? Be careful, tread lightly, don't reveal yourself, I said to myself, as do we all. For we are

3 primary controllers of behavior - stigma, gossip + rejection by family + friends,

bound like prisoners by certain social controls. Sociologists argue that stigma, gossip, and rejection by family and friends are among the most powerful of controls we encounter. We have a hard time being our authentic selves, even and especially with those persons who supposedly love us the most. And yet, as sociologists also tell us, it is the stranger with whom we often are most willing to be transparent.

One of our problems as Christians is that we may too readily confuse our experiences of being judged by other persons with our experiences and understandings of God. We project upon God the same reluctance to reveal ourselves that we present to others. We fear that God may reject us for reasons similar to those of family and friends. Beneath it all, sometimes tragically, we are besieged by internal conflicts about our own self-acceptance.

The fact is that the burden of self-shame is all too quickly conveyed to us from the moment we are born, whereupon the message we too often receive, hard-wired by negative reinforcement in the brain, is "I am of little or no worth." Sadly, this is the conclusion we come to about ourselves when most of all we need to hear instead the good news that God loves us and deems us to be of great worth despite all the falsities, pretenses, hypocrisies, and self-deceptions that plague our days.

I recently heard someone confess that it was no longer necessary to place the sole burden of blame for his adult struggles on the dysfunctions of his family of origin. For when taking a close look at his own marriage and family, he recognized a similar dysfunction being played out. The message he was passing on to his children sounded like this: Son—Daughter—don't do such-and-such a thing because of what people will think of you. Don't go over there to that particular place because people will glance at you with disapproval.

"Don't, don't, don't" was the repeated imperative. It was rooted in the dread of being judged and stigmatized by what others might think. The result was that the children began to shut down emotionally. Fears of verdicts from the outside prompted shrinking self-confidence and self-esteem on the inside.

When I was a kid, I used to ride my bike down the street and place into people's mailboxes little tract-like papers telling them how to find Jesus. But someone warned me that putting things into mailboxes was a federal offense and that I needed to stop. So I then went to the neighbor's house to tell her directly about Jesus. Yet when I knocked on the door her dog broke through the screen. I felt suddenly shame-bound for disrupting the elderly woman's life. Quickly I learned not to tell my story, even if the story was about Jesus.

You could say that this experience turned out to be the flip side of the parental "don't, don't, don't." For what I had heard as a child in church was "do, do, do." That is, do tell people about Jesus. Do talk about him. It's a good thing. But then, given what happened when I actually told someone about Jesus, embarrassment and shame set in.

This leads me to say a word about hypocrisy. We Evangelicals seem to have a knack for making each other feel guilty about our failure to tell the world about Jesus, while at the same time we go on saying to ourselves: You should pass out tracts. You should be a street preacher. You should pray with your neighbor. You should do something for somebody in need. You should . . . you should . . . you should.

As Evangelicals we seem bent upon hearing, talking about, and critiquing others' beliefs. But seldom do we do a good job of listening to each other's life-stories and validating one another as persons. Being fixated upon what we think others need to believe, we overlook what we most of all need for ourselves, which is affirmation of our self-worth in the eyes of God and one another.

The same is true about the self-worth of others. We displace our unworthy sense of self upon others by holding them to standards of "right belief" that we ourselves are far from measuring up to. This is what Jesus pointed out when calling the scribes and Pharisees to task: "They devour widows' houses and for the sake of appearance say long prayers" (Luke 20:47a). Their unjust treatment of widows made hypocrisy of their prayers. Piety provided no cover for their injustice. They had forgotten the words of one of their own prophets:

[handwritten: Critique of Israel's worship]

I hate, I despise your festivals, and I take no delight in
your solemn assembles. Even though you offer me your burnt
offerings and grain offerings, I will not accept them and the offering of well-being of your fatted animals I will not look upon.
Take away from me the noise of your songs; I will not listen to
the melody of your harps. But let justice roll down like water,
and righteousness like an everflowing stream. (Amos 5:21-24)

[handwritten right margin: lacking in justice]

[handwritten: God not impressed w/ it because of injustice]

Unfortunately, for many of us Evangelicals, "right beliefs" have become our public persona, the equivalent of long pharisaical prayers. We display our neatly bundled beliefs for others to see and adopt as their own. But what about our acts of justice and mercy? When we take an honest look at ourselves "just as we are," how do we measure up when it comes to our relationships with persons of color, LGBTQ persons, immigrant persons, and others? Do we treat them as any less worthy than we are of God's abundant acceptance and love? *[handwritten: Focus on right belief - Also single out]*

That is to say, if any such persons were to tell us their stories, saying to us, "Hear me 'just as I am,'" would we open ourselves to them without prejudice and with the same welcoming compassion that Jesus bears toward each one of us?—"Just as I am, without one plea, but that thy blood was shed for me"? *[handwritten: reflection]*

I often tell my students at the beginning of the semester to find a way to get "their voice out on the table," since together we do

To move things f. head to heart must tell stor. f.

not learn until we all have made our stories known. And that's because things will move from head to heart when we share our stories
and songs with one another. When I have heard their hearts and stop
worrying so much about what is in their heads, lo and behold, my
own soul's longing to share my story and sing my song "just as I am"
stirs within me.

In my sociology of religion course I recently tried something
different from my usual practice. I asked students to write their
religious autobiography, even if it was about growing up without
religion ("nones," meaning persons of no religion, is now an of-
ficial religious category for us sociologists). I told them that the
classroom is a safe place to tell their stories and to sing their songs,
and that we would not be critiquing or criticizing or judging one
another's deep-down sharing. Their stories were to be grounded
in their socialization, that is, in what they had learned, seen, and
experienced at home, in school, in religious settings, and elsewhere.
This was to be their time to reveal and explore together without
being judged.

The results were amazing—honest, raw, moving, and deeply
personal. As students listened to what sprang from the souls of others, the experience had a transformative effect upon their beliefs. One
person, who assumed that all Christians were right-wing supporters
of Donald Trump, had previously declared himself to be an atheist.
But having heard the stories of others, including Roman Catholics
and Evangelicals who believed in God, by the end of the semester he
said, "For the first time I now see that perhaps I can believe in God.
I need some time to think more about this."

It wasn't his hearing about the beliefs of those Christians that
opened his mind and heart, but rather it was hearing their deep-
down personal stories. As a result, I walked away from the semester
grieving that the church provides so few opportunities for such hon-

est conversations in which we silence our need to express our beliefs long enough to listen to another's heart.

One listener to the podcast responded with a note that I'm afraid far too often reflects what we hear in the church:

> I went to an "Apologetics Conference" a few years ago—before I had totally divested myself of all "corporate church" goings-on—and saw a number of big names speak. One was J. Warner Wallace, who concluded the final day of the conference by telling the audience (mostly high school and early college folks, and a few adults like me) that we needed to *stop* telling our personal stories! He made a deeply hammered point of the fact that "nobody cares about your story" and that we need to stop "giving our testimonies" and, instead, stick with the *facts* about the Bible being true, about the archaeological and ethical-logical arguments for the truth of the Bible. He said (with a bit of a sneer) that by sharing "our stories" we wouldn't win anyone over for Jesus. I found this (and many other things I heard at the conference), quite honestly, troubling and confusing, for when my heart has been changed by others it has been because they shared their *stories* and perspectives, and not because of the "cold hard facts."

From toddler to grownup, Sunday school is frequently too much about believing the right things and talking about doing the right things, yet rarely about enabling our children and ourselves as adults to integrate the gospel from the biblical stories, including the stories of Jesus, with truth-telling about ourselves. For Jesus enters our stories not as a belief but as a person. Just as God does, Jesus cares and listens to who we are, to what's going on with us, to how we're doing, to what we're facing and struggling with, to our deepest longings, hopes, desires, and, yes, to our darkest moments of despair.

"Just as I am, though tossed about with many a conflict, many a doubt, fightings and fears within, without, O Lamb of God, I come, I come."

When the church becomes a safe haven to tell our stories, we find far more growth occurring within our souls and ultimately much more love to offer one another. But when we are overly defended and protected by our beliefs, we miss the rich experiences of one another.

As with Truman Burbank in the movie "The Truman Show," the surrounding culture conditions us to live inauthentically within a walled reality, deprived of the fullness of true selfhood. Breaking away from those constraints, those walls, does not come easily, for we must first disabuse ourselves of the "believed reality" that disguises the truth about our common human condition. Truman believed from an early age that his father had been lost at sea, only to discover later with his very own eyes, and to his sudden shock, that his father lived as a homeless man on the street. We too require such moments of startling awakening. For it is then that we see what's transpiring not only within ourselves but also within others.

I wish I had broken through this kind of walled reality earlier in my life. I wish that doing so had not required the diagnosis of Parkinson's disease, which confronted me with the fact that my days were numbered, and that if ever I wanted to become an honestly authentic human being, then I'd better start now. I wish I had cared far less about what other saints and sinners (we're all a mix of both) had thought of me, and about what I *believed* of what they thought of me. For I knew what no one else could possibly know about me until I shared it, which is the truth of my own deep-down story.

By God's grace, and with thanksgiving, I finally broke through the wall. Yes, it's better to arrive home late than not at all. It's better to live authentically for a short time than to live inauthentically all of the time. Such breakthroughs, I believe, are God's way of preparing us to live in the richness and fullness of God's kingdom that, yes, begins now.

It's better for God to undertake the hard work of sanctification within me now rather than at the last minute when I stand before him, smoking like smoldering straw rather than bearing a golden crown. Or, as St. Paul said plainly enough, "Work out your own salvation with fear and trembling; for it is God who is at work in you, enabling you both to will and to work for his good pleasure" (Phil 2:12b).

As for God's good pleasure, if ever I were to have the privilege of hearing the story of that listener to my podcast, who seemed so disgruntled by what he heard of my story, I pray that I should be able to accept his story and his song—the holy truth of it—from deep-down within him, with grace and without judgment.

"Blessed assurance . . . This is my story, this is my song."

PART TWO

A CHURCH
DISMANTLED

CHAPTER THREE

Why the Church Cannot Re-open
May 2020

Several months into the Covid pandemic, this chapter was the first of what would become the podcast "A Church Dismantled—A Kingdom Restored." The essay was originally one of my so-called "Weekly Emails" to our local congregation where my wife Heidi and I lead together.

Nearly everywhere we turn these days we are hearing the word "re-open": re-open the country, re-open the economy, re-open nail salons, restaurants, barbershops, gyms, major league baseball, and just about everything else we've done without for the last two months. And now, more and more we are hearing that it is time to "re-open the church." The problem is that the Church cannot be re-opened, for the Church was never, ever closed.

The idea that churches can be "re-opened" along with barbershops and malls and hair salons reveals our concept of ecclesiology and our theological orientation as twenty-first century Americans, namely, that congregations are places to go to consume religious goods and to shop for various expressions of worship, preaching, and community that best fit our lifestyles, our preferences, and our theology (to the extent that any of us are thoughtful anymore about the latter).

But the Church is not a barbershop or a restaurant that can be opened and closed. The Church (capital "C") is a living and breathing organism, the very body of our Lord Jesus Christ, of which he is the head. The fact that the wooden doors to our church buildings may never open again will have nothing to do with God's eschatology—the new heaven and new earth for which the Lord of history is shaping the future.

The problem with rushing to "re-open the church" is that we may sabotage the work that the Holy Spirit is wishing to do among us/in this time of "dis-assembly." After all, Jesus instructed his disciples to wait for forty days for the coming of the Holy Spirit at Pentecost. What a shame it would be to miss the coming of God's Spirit in new ways in this time by our impatience to return to a previous reality that has served God's purposes in the past but may not be well suited for the future that God is building.

Fifteen years ago, while writing *Road Signs for the Journey*, I sensed a question that by now I've come to believe came from the Holy Spirit: What if the Spirit is dismantling the church, so that once again, here and now, we can get on with God's mission in the world that "God so loved" and so loves still? As I've asked that question in various settings in recent years, it has resonated with many persons, perhaps because it has become abundantly clear that God is dismantling the church of *our creation*, but not the Church reflecting the "pure and spotless bride of Christ" that God intends us to be.

So, before we jump the gun and attempt to go back to something that may already be gone, let's lean into God's Spirit to discern in the presence of Christ what exactly we are to "move into" and "create anew," rather than "move back to" in an "embrace of the old." For I am quite confident that there is no moving back or embracing of an "old" that we previously created. By God's grace, the old has become history.

In our own congregation, as we show up on Zoom together, there is an authenticity and freedom that has come to all of us as we feel less pressure to "perform" and "dress up to go to church." Whatever the future of our congregation turns out to look like, I pray that we never regress to that "Egypt" where "going to church" means leaving our genuine selves behind so that for two hours a week we can be what we think others, or our "socially constructed" views of God, expect of us.[5] If that isn't bondage, then I don't know what is.

Frankly, my hope and prayer is that whenever we re-assemble face-to-face, it will be only after God has had the chance to do his holy, transformative work within us individually and corporately.

---

[5]   I will use the phrase "social construction" or the "social construction of reality" throughout this book. It is a sociological term that simply means that society and our social worlds "create" our realities for us. They may or may not be true realities but they appear as true to us because others have told us they are true and we come to accept these realities as normative. The best sociological source for further reading about this concept is Peter L. Berger and Thomas Luckmann, *The Social Construction of Reality* (New York: Vintage Books, 1966).

CHAPTER FOUR

When Re-opening Just Might Be Our Closing
May 2020

A s with the people of Babel and the Israelites within the Pharisaical tradition, the modern world depends upon being held together by four defining characteristics—counting things, predicting things, controlling things, and doing things—as quickly and efficiently as possible.[6] The Covid-19 crisis has brought modernity to its knees just as God lowered the boom on Babel and just as Jesus so frequently turned upside down the "taken-for-granted reality" of the Pharisees.[7] At the moment, there is nothing rationally predictable about the coronavirus, nothing foolproof we have found to control it or effectively treat it, and no way to measure with certainty who has

---

[6] In his book *The McDonaldization of Society* (California: Pine Forge Press, 1993), social theorist George Ritzer addresses the qualities of "modernity" or what we mean when we describe the modern world. Throughout the book you will hear me describe the "formal rationality" of the modern world, by which we mean that the world is organized in efficient and bureaucratic ways and through social institutions such as government, the economy, education, religion, health care, and more. These institutions are organized in ways that have come to "make sense" to us and that are largely structured according to formal rules, procedures, and regulations or what we often call "red tape." Formal rationality has come to dominate modernity as predicted a century ago by German sociologist Max Weber, who argued that the bureaucracies resulting from such rationality would lead to all of us being captured within an "iron cage of rationality." Max Weber, *Economy and Society* (Cambridge: Harvard University Press, 2019 [1922]).

Again, Berger and Luckmann, *The Social Construction of Reality*, are the authors who emphasized that we human beings construct social worlds that in turn "construct" us.

Enlightment worldview displace
Mystery w/ Rationality + Empiricism

it and who doesn't. In other words, the rationality of modern life has not yet proven to be sufficient to overcome this pandemic.

The coronavirus appears to have undone many of the assumptions that our modern predisposition for certainty is built upon, which is to say, an Enlightenment worldview that displaces God with science, faith with empiricism, and the heart with a rationalistic and sometimes rationalizing mind. Subtly but surely, the cultural fog of inevitable human progress emanating from the last several centuries has swept over the church. And so, the church—like barbershops, hair salons, restaurants, and everything else we presently want to see re-opened—has fashioned itself into a little tower of Babel resting upon the shifting sands of counting things, predicting things, controlling things, and doing things altogether as efficiently as humanly possible.

But what if the coronavirus, reflecting as it does the unpredictability and inefficiency of the Holy Spirit, has been visited upon us by the Creator, much like the plagues of ancient Egypt, to challenge the false belief that we are in control, and for the purpose of addressing our failure to rely upon God as the Lord of both the present and the future?

What if, in our rush to re-open the church, just as the world around us rushes to re-open bars, barbershops, and hair salons, we actually turn away from the work of the Holy Spirit among us? What if the rush to re-open is driven by our reflexive desire to control the mission of God by fashioning it to our comforts, such as the predictability of our worship and programmatic services? What if the money coming once again into our coffers is to cover the cost of maintaining buildings and staff salaries, yet only for the sake of returning to efficiencies that promise to offset the inefficiencies we are now experiencing?

As human beings, we rarely learn when we are at ease with our experience. Rather, we learn from being thrown into the whirlwind,

Learn When Worlds are turned to pos, turvy

the calamity, or the predicament in which we must reflect upon and reconsider our commitments. The fall of Babel's tower left carnage in its wake. But were those who shuffled through its rubble any wiser for God's having "scattered them abroad"? And to what end? That they might reorient themselves? If so, then from what, to what? From fixation upon their humanly built "tower with its top in the heavens," to the immortal will and way of the God who had wreaked havoc upon their pride?

As Christians, are we not being summoned, above all else, to discern the mind of Christ, and what it is that Christ is saying to us in the here and now of our coronaviral scatteredness and isolation?

I would suggest that the question for all of us is not "When will God return the kingdom to Israel?" in the form of some homesick "normalcy" to re-opened churches, but instead, how shall we make sure we don't miss what the Holy Spirit is doing in our midst, by breaking us of our tendency to predict, count, control, and be efficient?

I don't think we have yet had enough time even to begin prayerfully to reflect upon that question. If the rebuilding of Babel is what we are up to—by putting back into place traditions that, as once before in "Israel," are what Jesus called cracked and leaky wineskins—then we are engaged in acts of self-defeating futility.

Just as the psalmist of Psalm 46, who in his time beheld the "desolations" that God "has brought on the earth," we too in our time of desolation are called to "be still and know that I am God." I don't know about you, but I know that over these past three months I have not begun to be still enough yet to know what God is up to in his cosmic undoing of the modern world as we have come to know it—and in his undoing of the church which in far too many instances we have re-created in our own cultural images.

CHAPTER FIVE

Malls and Megachurches: Covid-Crisis Casualties?
May 2020

Evangelical churches have long assumed that we were safe from the declines affecting our mainline cousins—Presbyterians, Methodists, Anglicans, Episcopalians, and Lutherans, among others. We assumed that their decline of membership and attendance resulted from their embrace of a progressive theology rooted in Enlightenment rationality and its empirical products. God was placed under the microscope and the Bible under the lens of literary criticism, and both came up short. Whatever the mainline offered, its children could invariably find something else of greater meaning in the world. And so, as the mainline church followed its children into the enticing sights and sounds of the surrounding culture, it increasingly disappeared into that world with them.

We Evangelicals thought we were safe. To ensure this, we built bigger churches with better "products." We became more "professional" and offered our members a predictable and efficient diet of goods and services without demanding too much in return for fear that our children, like those of the mainline, might also leave the church for the world.

Little did we know that to be modern had as much to do with how we structured and comported ourselves as it did with what we believed. In constructing an efficient, predictable religious experience, which we could count upon and control, we were destroying any remaining fabric of authentic faith community that some religious bodies historically had been known for embodying. We were as much at risk as the mainline, subject to falling prey to the lure of modernity.

While believing we could look the other way, the Enlightenment nevertheless brought with it not only rational beliefs but also rational structures—efficient, predictable ones that we could count upon and control, yet just as fragile as a theology without God or the Bible. If the mainline has lacked a prescient theology sufficiently equipped to explain if not subdue a virus created to attack every aspect of modernity, then most of us who claim some kinship to evangelicalism seem now to lack the constitutive strength and purpose of an enduring community capable of withstanding the onslaught of the current Covid crisis.

As a result, if the church is principally little more than a place to go on Sunday to hang our caps and jackets on the coat rack and take our seats in the pew to relieve a lengthy bout of pandemic loneliness and isolation, then we had better "get it open" and "get on with it" in a hurry. Otherwise, like the teetering tower of Babel, our present inability to "be still and know that I am God" may cause our loneliness and isolation to come crashing down all around and over us.

CHAPTER SIX

If the Spirit's Dismantling the Church, How Can I Help?

May 2020

In an earlier post in 2007, I had asked the question: What if the Spirit is dismantling the church? By now in 2020, I think it has become pretty clear that this indeed may be what the Spirit is up to, person-by-person if not stone-by-stone as with the dismantling of the city of Jerusalem and its temple shrine at the hands of Nebuchadnezzar in Jeremiah's time.

I'm not sure why we are quick to assume that the Spirit of the living God would never do such a thing to the church today, when God was so amenable to the destruction of the sixth-century-BC temple, including its Holy of Holies where God's very presence was deemed foremost to dwell.

Does God not have a grand history of tearing down and starting from scratch, of destroying in order to begin again—with the great flood of Noah's epoch and the Babylonian exile being but two instances within Hebrew scripture, in addition to the fiery destruction of Herod's temple in AD 70, which Jesus himself had predicted? Indeed, when God called Jeremiah, he did so "to pluck up and to pull down, to destroy and to overthrow, to build and to plant" (Jer 1:10).

The apostle Paul declared that our mortal physical bodies are also "temples" in which through our Lord's death and resurrection God's spirit dwells. What then of our mortal ecclesiastical "bodies"? Are they not also holy places whose life, as Jesus said, we must lose in order to gain life? The divine dismantling, it would appear, occurs when we construct our "worlds" in ways that get in the way of God's way for this world and all of God's creatures in it. For it is God who plucks up and pulls down, destroys and overthrows, builds and plants. Or do we not believe that to be so anymore?

Having posed the question—what if God's Spirit is dismantling the church?—I followed with another: How then do we work with the Spirit rather than against the Spirit? For the Spirit's work is the work of every saint in every given time.

When I was a kid, I bought a little book called *Freeway under Construction* by Judson Cornwall.[8] Over the years, I read and reread what it said from a Pentecostal perspective, long before I had any idea of what Pentecostal meant. The pages grabbed my soul. For they described God's grand excavation project in the book of the prophet Isaiah:

> A voice cries out: "In the wilderness prepare the way of the Lord, make straight in the desert a highway for our God. Every valley shall be lifted up, and every mountain and hill be made low; the uneven ground shall become level, and the rough places a plain. The glory of the Lord shall be revealed, all people shall see it together, for the mouth of the Lord has spoken." (Isa 40:1–5)

Folks, the voice crying out in the wilderness cries for us. For we are called to be part of the most exciting excavation project in all of history, side by side with the Holy Spirit: Tearing down the things we have built that block the thoroughfare to God's kingdom. Raising the valleys where the secrets of God have been forgotten and God's ancient paths hidden by human overgrowth. Making the

---

8   Judson Cornwall, *Freeway under Construction* (Bellingham: Logos, 1978). https://www.amazon.com/Freeway-under-construction-Judson-Cornwall/dp/0882703048/.

rough ground level and the rugged places a plain. Why? So that all may experience the glory of God.

By now it is clear to me that I believe the church as we have created it, like the excesses of Solomon's temple and everything by way of idolatry that God's people took to be sacred in Jeremiah's day, is in the process of being dismantled and rebuilt in a new way for a new day.

As I observe the responses to my Facebook posts over the last two weeks, it is apparent that we have created a church that makes it difficult for people to find onramps to the King's highway. How is this so?

It's because of our shared "church" culture, our inside jokes, our rejection of society's discarded persons who belong nevertheless to the very world of God's making that we are called upon to serve. It's because of our focus on church buildings as the primary locus of where church happens, and our irreverent assumption that only our own kind of special people are called to minister, rather than a host of ordinary souls of every gender and skin tone whom God calls to minister. All of these troubling considerations raise another serious question. Where does our *faithlessness* end, and where does God's *faithfulness* begin?

Isaiah provides the answer in prophetic picture-words, words that later fell from the very lips of Jesus. For it is God's faithfulness that upends the world's faithlessness. It is God's purpose:

Churches Miss

To bring good news to the oppressed, to bind up the brokenhearted, to proclaim liberty to the captives, and release to the prisoners; to proclaim the year of the Lord's favor . . . to comfort all who mourn . . . to give them a garland instead of ashes, the oil of gladness instead of mourning, the mantle of praise instead of a faint spirit. . . They shall build up the ancient ruins, they shall raise up the former devastations; they shall repair the ruined cities, the devastations of many generations. (Isa 61:1b–4; cf. Luke 4:18–19)

I think, for instance, of an especially egregious devastation, which is America's original sin of racism and the corrupted and darkened heart of white supremacy that has inflicted crushing cruelties, flagrant injustices, and gross inequities for four hundred years now.

In contrast, Jesus hung out with persons whose lives languished on the margins and teetered on the brink, wounded by the jagged edges of others' pride and privilege. He did so not because he pitied them but because he loved them. He felt so much more at home with the outcast and the outsider than with those who spiritually preened and pruned themselves with burnt offerings that quickly went up in smoke within the socially rarified and segregated courts of the temple. In contrast, while pouring out the coins and overturning the tables of the moneychangers, Jesus declared: "Is it not written, 'My house shall be called a house of prayer for all the nations'? But you have made it a den of robbers" (Mark 11:17; cf. Isa 56:7c).

The divine dismantling during this time of pandemic may be a moment of *kairos*—a crucial time when conditions are right—when God is giving God's people an occasion for pausing to reflect and consider: "How do we work with the Spirit rather than against the Spirit?"

Rushing back to church to reinforce what we fear may be imminently falling apart, or to salvage what we unfortunately are misled to believe the government may surreptitiously be taking from us, is not the path forward in this present wilderness—lest in doing so we lose our souls in the rubble of God's disassembly of the old order. For God is building a new order. "See," he says, "I am making all things new" (Rev 21:5).

The Church, as God recreates it, is never closed and never shall be. "Knock, and the door will be opened for you" (Matt 7:7).

CHAPTER SEVEN

The Spirit Is Coming—But I Want to Go Back to Church First!
May 2020

Jesus has just spent three arduous years forming and preparing his disciples to carry on with spreading the good news of God's kingdom, so that the blind may see, the lame walk, and the oppressed be set free—by proclaiming the fullness of God's grace and goodness for which the human heart most yearns.

And now, summoning them again to the task at hand, as he is about to take leave of them, he announces that they will not be left alone to carry out his monumental mission on their own. "I will ask the Father, and he will give you another Advocate, to be with you forever" (John 14:16). The gift of the Holy Spirit is to become theirs, to equip and empower them for what lies ahead. He promises, "I will not leave you orphaned; I am coming to you" (v. 18).

But the disciples are neither attuned to the Spirit nor focused upon the work that Jesus has set before them. They are looking backward. Before they even begin to hear what Jesus is saying to them, they are dead-set upon returning, as we would say, "to church." Back to the way things used to be. Back to those glorious moments we remember so fondly, before Jesus set his face toward Jerusalem and the prospect of his gruesome execution upon a Roman cross.

Like the disciples, who presumably knew Jesus best, we too show little zeal for the rigors of his kingdom and the assurances that his Spirit is with us. For the most part, just as they, we misunderstand him in spite of the fact that he declares to us: "In a little while the world will no longer see me, but you will see me; because I live, you also will live" (v. 19). His words are spoken in the future tense, not the past tense. Yet because the future remains unknown, we look back in lament over what has passed and gone, and with longing for its impossible rejuvenation.

The problem with the rear-view mirror is that we repress the painful parts of the past while romanticizing the best parts—delighting in those quaint memories of the rationed food we ate while we were slaves in Egypt, yet forgetting the scorching heat we endured beneath the pounding sun when as his subjects we were forced to bake Pharoah's bricks out of clay and take the lashes of his taskmasters' whips to our backs.

When the world, as we once knew it for all of its fleeting goodness, suddenly disappears, as it always does, there is no way that wishful thinking will retrieve it as a more perfect world than it actually was.

Some days, when our desert oasis dries up, and the locusts descend, and the flowers wither, we simply have to fold up our tents and move on, lest we perish in the blinding, windswept sands. Or, as the case happens to be during this year of pandemic, for now we stay put and hunkered down in our tents with our knees creased upon the ground and the palms of our hands slanted upward toward the heavens.

Then, when the all-clear signal is given to us desert pilgrims to gather once again, we discover that, this time around, it is to where night storms have torn asunder the rooftops, sunrays have bleached warp into the wood, cobwebs have covered the pew racks, and rusty nails have jutted through the doorsteps to dissuade us of ever thinking we are stepping back into the good old times.

In *Road Signs for the Journey*, I wagered that a Babel-like dispersion might be what we in the church most need to kick-start us out of an un-Spirited complacency. If this world-scale Covid pandemic has not in fact done so, by shattering all manner of business as usual, thereby arousing radical spiritual renewal, then I'm not sure what would do so for the sake of this present moment and the future.

The problem with looking in the rearview mirror is that we can't see what's coming at us. Jesus always points his disciples to the new reality—God's future breaking through to us and upon us. How tragic if we miss it for having our heads turned the other way!

So, I am left with a few questions. And I would ask you, what are yours?

What if the visitation of the Holy Spirit draws us only forward, not backward?

What if the Spirit seeks to revivify our homes and marriages and families and cities and neighborhoods before, not after, we point our feet "back to church"?

What if the experience of Pentecost, this time around, seizes our houses and apartment complexes when heretofore it has seemed to by-pass our church edifices?

What if the breezes from God's heaven invade our dwelling places to sweep out the demons from hell that reside crouching among the ghosts of the past that inhabit every troubled room?

Might the Spirit prompt us to switch the channels we watch, the books we read, and the words we speak? Which is to say, alter the way we live?

What if the church, as it once was, is not the church the Spirit is remaking us to be now? Us as the church! Not simply our buildings, but us!

According to the prophet Jeremiah, one of Yahweh-God's searing critiques of his people, who too often thoroughly exasperated him, was that "they did not say, 'Where is the Lord?'"

"They did not say, 'Where is the Lord who brought us up from the land of Egypt, who led us in the wilderness, in a land of deserts and pits, in a land of draught and deep darkness, in a land that no one passes through, where no one lives?'" (Jer 2:6).

"Where is the Lord" *now*? That must be our question.

Among all of the pandemic-driven conversations that I have heard about when and how we should go back to church, I have not heard much by way of asking, "Where is the Lord?"

Through the prophecy of Jeremiah, the Lord pled with his people: "Stand at the crossroads and look; ask for the ancient paths, ask where the good way is and walk in it" (6:16). Yet, to you and me, to "ask for the ancient paths" may seem to contradict everything I've said up to this point. Except for one thing.

Whenever we ask: "Where is the Lord?" and, "Where are those ancient paths?"—God and God's paths are never behind us. They are always in front of us. For that is where the Spirit of God-in-Christ dwells and travels, with us, as if for the very first time. For so it will always seem as though it is for the very first time, in as much as nothing for long remains the same. Not even "church."

Once again, says the Lord: "See, I am making all things new" (Rev 21:5). "I will not leave you orphaned; I am coming to you" (John 14:18).

CHAPTER EIGHT

With Wind and Fire, Yes—
But with a Novel Coronavirus?
May 2020

Still in a daze over Jesus's failure to give them a good answer about when they could go back to "church," that is, back to things as normal, the disciples ended up "together in one place" (Acts 2:1).

Suddenly from out of nowhere, or as Luke puts it in the book of Acts, "a sound like the rush of a violent wind . . . filled the entire house where they were sitting," and "divided tongues, as of fire, appeared among them, and a tongue rested on each of them" (vv. 2–3).

Perhaps such an order of wind and fire comprises the height of revival we need today. Could that be so? For as long as I can remember, I've heard a repeated cry for "revival, revival, revival."

It's hard to argue against revival as a Christian, isn't it? We all know that if we were to do so, that some well-meaning saint would surely give us the "what-for." Baseball, apple pie, and revival—who could possibly be against them?

The problem is that revivals, from the preacher's point of view, are to be directed mostly toward someone else. We preachers may have a hard time admitting that "revival" needs to begin with us. Notwithstanding our misappropriation of that term, who will remain behind the altar to pray for all of those sinners and backsliders if we the preachers walk forward to stand in front of the altar as one of them? For then we would have to leave the praying up to Jesus!

In addition, revivalism often possesses an air of grand spectacle, whereby it promises a kind of catch-one-catch-all, tame-one-tame-all panacea that makes us feel better about ourselves for the moment, having revved ourselves into a frenzy without changing much of anything about the way we are living. We put on the veil of righteousness without being washed and scrubbed of the grit and grime beneath the veil.

If we hold fast to the idea that revival awaits us "out there" somewhere in the distant future, whence it will magically emerge in God's good time, and with little or no effort on our part, then we can act as though we are relieved of all immediate responsibility to "work out [our] own salvation in fear and trembling," as Saint Paul says (Phil 2:12). We can go on living like the devil until that day when heaven's curtain is drawn back upon a far greater spectacle than a tent revival meeting.

I remember as a child sitting in Sunday School at Locust Grove Mennonite Church, with my teacher telling us how bad the world was *out there*. And I recall myself thinking, teacher, the badness might be out there but it's also *in here*, in this church, in this heart. Because these four walls don't keep the devil out.

So, what keeps the devil out? Life with God. Life from God. A lifetime devoted to God. Deep prayer and deep reading of the Word of God. Being deeply situated in the presence of God.

As much as you or I may wish for the rush of a tornadic wind and the burst of flaming tongues of fire to descend upon the night-fog of our existence (I would never diminish that possibility!), there is nonetheless something about the divine Spirit (*ruach*, Hebrew: "breath" of God), being the very same "wind from God that swept over the face of the waters" (Gen 1:2), taking its own good time, eons perhaps, not by rationing God's presence a morsel at a time but by working within our spirits a scrap at a time—until—we surrender to God's will, in spite of ourselves.

Consider, then, that the church—the "temple"—is precisely wherever you and I happen to be for now. "Do you not know that you are God's temple and that God's Spirit dwells in you?" (1 Cor 3:16). Does this not mean that we are never without God no matter where we are?

What is the most crucial thing in the course of the average day that we are most prone to forget? Isn't it that from our birth to the present moment we are deeply situated within the presence of God? Have we forgotten? Do we see? Do we hear? Do we acknowledge? Do we give thanks?

The Spirit's descent at Pentecost made Peter a bold preacher for one day, yet it would take the Spirit's further work, through a bit of cajoling by his fellow apostle Paul, to overcome Peter's resistance to the truth that the good news of God's salvation is that God is present to all people. Emphasis *all*.

So, what happened on that "Pentecost Day" when Jesus stood next to the well, talking with a woman? She asked, "How is it that you, a Jew, ask a drink of me, a woman of Samaria?" (John 4:4–30). For it wasn't supposed to happen that way. First, he shouldn't have been talking with a woman in public. Second, there was virtually nothing normally conveyed between Jews and Samaritans by way of good news, since more often than not they were enemies.

"Jesus answered her, 'If you knew the gift of God, and who it is that is saying to you, "Give me a drink," you would have asked him, and he would have given you living water'" (v. 10). And, when he did give her living water, she heard, she saw, she "drank," and she gave thanks.

Then, too, what happened on that "Pentecost Day" when Jesus came to a full stop beneath a sycamore tree to invite himself into the house of the despised tax collector Zacchaeus (Luke 19:1–10)?

And, on that "Pentecost Day" when the woman who sought to be released from twelve years of hemorrhaging touched the "fringe of his cloak" (Matt 9:20–22)?

And, on that "Pentecost Day" when Jesus drew near the Gerasene demoniac, whose name was "Legion," who languished among the tombs and grumbled, "What have you to do with me, Jesus, Son of the Most High God?" (Mark 5:1–13)?

For what happens on all such "Pentecost Days"?—as when on the first Pentecost, being

> amazed and astonished, they asked, "Are not all these who are speaking Galileans? And how is it that we hear, each of us, in our own native language? Parthians, Medes, Elamites, and residents of Mesopotamia, Judea and Cappadocia, Pontus and Asia, Phrygia and Pamphylia, Egypt and the parts of Libya belonging to Cyrene, and visitors from Rome, both Jews and proselytes, Cretans and Arabs—in our own languages we hear them speaking about God's deeds of power." All were amazed and perplexed, saying to one another, "What does this mean?" (Acts 2:7–12)

Did all of them not see? hear? and give thanks?

Most did. "Others sneered and said, 'They are filled with new wine'" (vs. 13).

It may seem like a bizarre twist of Pentecost, but I've been wondering of late if the Spirit may have come around this time, with the novel coronavirus in tow, as the occasion for reviving the wind and fire of our universal creaturehood, brotherhood, and sisterhood—lest we earthlings think for a moment that we can accomplish this viral task of "living together" in mutual peace and harmony apart from the very presence of God who daily and nightly breathes life into us. Into all of us.

The Spirit of God some days is like the morning mist, other days like the blazing sun, moving within and about all our days, and not a single one of them set apart from the Spirit.

Sometimes wind. Sometimes fire. Sometimes the "still, small voice."

Do we see? Do we hear? Do we give thanks?

CHAPTER NINE

Spirit and Savior: The Best "Two-for-One" Special Ever
May 2020

It's strange that growing up well into my adulthood I thought the Spirit to be a completely different species, divorced from Jesus. I imagined Jesus as a kind and gentle shepherd, the one who invited children to come to him without hindrance, the one who died for my sins and made me his child, the one who made the lame walk and the blind see. But the Spirit? A different species?

I grew up deathly afraid of the Holy Spirit, sure that day-after-day I had committed the unpardonable sin of blaspheming the Spirit. I often believed that though Jesus loved me and had forgiven me, I had so offended the Spirit that my salvation was thereby invalidated. I was a goner—headed for hell despite anything Jesus said or did—and all because I had sinned against the Spirit whom Jesus had left behind himself as a hound to test my faithfulness.

While I knew that Christ Jesus had indeed lived and died for my salvation, it wasn't clear to me just why the Spirit had come. So, I did my level-best to develop a theology that excluded the Spirit. Consequently, whenever I thought I had committed blasphemy, that sin above of all sins, I would once again ask Jesus to be my Savior and start the salvation process all over again. Though my particular struggles and inner terror concerning the Holy Spirit may have seemed in greater abundance than for other Christians, I do not believe that it was my twisted thinking alone that made this so. Many who claimed to be followers of Jesus seemed to me also to have concocted the same Spirit-lite or Spirit-less theology.

Of course, none of us would likely admit to such impoverishment, for who of us could not recite the Apostles' Creed as evidence of our belief? "I believe . . . in the Holy Ghost." But the difference between our beliefs and the practices we devote to them can be problematic enough to impact our eternal wellbeing. Just so, at times demonic forces also are infused with beliefs.

The so-called twentieth-century "German Christians," who religiously recited the Apostles' Creed on Sundays, also saluted the racist, anti-Semitic ideology of Adolf Hitler, which led to Jews and others being "boxcarred" by train to the infamous Nazi concentration camps and gas chambers—a perennially dangerous ideology to which American Christianity is not impervious.

Hitler took lessons directly from the United States' Jim Crow anti-miscegenation and segregation laws, as well as from the 1924 Immigration Act that turned away southern and eastern Europeans and Asians from our borders while admitting northern Europeans. These American heresies became the basis for Germany's Nuremburg Laws that barred Jewish citizenship.

Not so very long ago, some White American Christians, no less, ostensibly worshipped God's Spirit on Sundays and then gathered in bands of the devil on Mondays beneath the lynching tree, to hang Black bodies and strip them of the Spirit's life. Not all human spirits are of God's Spirit. For such racist theology is devoid of the Spirit.

This business of divorcing the Spirit from Jesus creates great trouble for us. It leaves us vulnerable to crisis after crisis in which we may easily fall prey to the surrounding demons that roam not so far from "the madding crowd."

Looking back, I must have had some unconscious sense that I needed the Spirit more than I knew I did. For, in 1982, I received a telephone call from someone at the Philadelphia College of the Bible, where I planned to enroll as a student in the fall. However, I returned my application materials without signing the belief statement because it was "cessationist," that is, it required a theological position that excluded the charismatic gifts of the Spirit.

While to my knowledge I had not experienced those charismatic gifts directly, and fearing just what the Spirit's coming into my life might portend, nevertheless I believed what the Bible said. From all that I could tell from reading it, there was nothing within it to suggest that healings, tongues, prophecies, and other charismatic gifts were no longer in play.

The person on the other end of the phone had sought to negotiate an arrangement with me. But my mind was settled. Any college that excluded the gifts of the Spirit was not a place for me. So, I exercised plan B and applied to Wheaton College where I was accepted.

It was approximately five years ago that I preached a sermon series about what I had learned that had completely transformed my understanding of the Spirit, namely that the Holy Spirit is not to be considered a separate species from Jesus. The Spirit is one with Jesus, as Jesus is one with God. During his lifetime in the flesh, Jesus didn't present the Spirit as divorced from himself but rather as part and parcel of who he was.

Concerning Jesus,

> John [the Baptist] testified, "I saw the Spirit descending from heaven like a dove, and it remained on him. I myself did not know him, but the one who sent me to baptize with water said to me, 'He on whom you see the Spirit descend and remain is the one who baptizes with the Holy Spirit.' And I myself have seen and have testified that this is the Son of God." (John 1:32–34)

What I finally came to realize was that Jesus's incarnation in the flesh was not only for my salvation and the forgiveness of my sins. It was to empower me to live in the Spirit and thereby be cleansed of the darkness surrounding my life and the world! Jesus prayed as much to the Father: "I made your name known to them, and I will make it known, so that the love with which you have loved me may be in them, and I in them" (17:26).

Paul put it this way: "But when the fullness of time had come, God sent his Son, born of a woman, born under the law, in order to redeem those who were under the law, so that we might receive adoption as children. And because you are children, God has sent the Spirit of his Son into our hearts, crying, 'Abba! Father!'" (Gal 4:4–6).

There it is! The "Spirit of his Son into our hearts"—Pentecost Day! By Christ's Spirit coming to us we are delivered from the clutches of death and darkness and self-deception, for the sake of our new beginning.

As I witness many of us, brothers and sisters, caught up in bitter political bantering over face masks and social distancing, and much more, it seems evident that we may have forgotten that we are children of the Spirit who dwells within us to bring light and life to an afflicted and anxious world.

So, we must ask ourselves: Have we opened, or have we shut, our doors to the Spirit? It's a question we do well to answer before we ever set foot again in the church building.

PART THREE

SINS OF A CHURCH
DISMANTLED

CHAPTER TEN

"Just as I Am" for the Great "I AM"?
May 2020

A s a kid, no melody made my stomach churn more than the hymn "Just as I am." We sang it mostly at tent revivals held during the sweltering months of summer. The heat and smell of canvas seemed like salt added to beads of perspiration, a reminder of the consequence of failing to "come down the aisle" during the preacher's invitation as the altar song resounded like the tune of a rusty old wire brush scratching its bristles against the rippled tin metal of a kitchen washboard. The tent, sad to say, was all too often a muggy place with the grass trodden down, itself in need of revival.

We routinely gathered to hear George Brunk II, a traveling Mennonite revivalist and divine mercenary of sorts, sent to the hinterland to rekindle us of the fact that we were not yet right with the Lord, and that this was surely our last chance to set things straight.

At least that's how it felt to my kid-like heart. And George was every bit the guy for the job—large man with deep voice—a heap of a soul—and exactly the kind I imagined God would commission to lay layers of gold thicker than tar on me "just as I am" since I was not yet all right with the Almighty "I AM." I mean, can you imagine God having sent a short skinny mouse of a man with a squeaky voice, intimidating the hell out of us for the sake of our someday making it, against all odds, to heaven?

It always felt like the altar call was orchestrated especially for me. To be honest, the customary invitation and accompanying RSVP were usually generic enough to snag just about any passer-by with a tad of conscience.

George's script: "If you are aware that you have fallen short . . ." (I was well aware). "If you have already asked Christ into your heart but have need to rededicate your life again . . ." (Just how would I know?). "If you harbor sin in your life that you are not sure you have confessed . . ." (I was perennially unsure). "If you came tonight uncertain about where you would go if you died tonight . . ." (I was nightly, weekly, monthly, and forever uncertain, despite my many pleas for Christ to enter my heart). "If you are unsure whether all of your sins are forgiven . . ." (All of them? Has God overlooked some?). "If you are holding a grudge or harboring bitterness toward another person . . ." (Are there any souls in this hot tent not sweating the recitation of their names on Judgment Day?). Well, you've got the drift.

Then there was that dreaded finale: "I'm going to wait just five more minutes . . . for I sense there's one more person . . ." (How come he always looked in my direction?) "One more person resisting God's Spirit, for whom this might be the last chance to escape hell's clutches. . ." (Heck, I'm already in George's clutches. Isn't that enough?) "I'll wait just five more minutes!" (A minute to George was twenty to me).

I really did have to wonder. Had God promised George a commission? Or maybe a double commission for this one, which was the singularly most mortifying trick taught every budding revivalist in revival school: "If you want to give your life, or rededicate your life to Christ, why, just slip your hand up right where you are. No one will notice you. This is just between you and God!"

Then to my horror, I heard the preacher add this: "Now, if you raised your hand, then I ask you to come to the front here and kneel at the altar!" And if I succumbed, then came the low whispers: "There goes that backslidden kid again." On the other hand, if I flaked out, then the *loud* whispers: "Why, that kid's just lying to himself if he thinks he doesn't need to kneel down before the Almighty!"

What I could never figure out, though, was why so few folks joined me at the altar when I did go up to stand before it. I mean, if you didn't fall into one of those "If you" categories that George set forth like Moses with his "Thou shalt nots" at Sinai, then what in the world were you or anybody else doing at a revival meeting? Or, was that torrid tent simply full of a bunch of hypocrites, including me? What was true, for sure, was that I was no saint worthy of heaven. And since I certainly didn't want to be named among the hypocrites, up the aisle I went.

But then there were those wretched backsliders—the ones the revivals were really intended for, to straighten them out. And we all knew who they were—usually the single guys, including every Johnny-come-lately who slid under the back flap of the tent. Just why they always seemed to be unmarried men was a mystery to me, other than for the fact that, generally speaking, people assumed there was an awful lot of trouble a single guy could get himself into in the valley.

I'm glad the tent revivals are now behind me. They were not helpful to my life with God. Probably they were helpful to some, and I suspect there were folks who found their way to Jesus because of George's faithfulness. It's just that terror and guilt are not great motivators in the long haul. Oh, those threats can get your child to do whatever you want for a while, but they usually accumulate resentment and shame, both of which are more likely to convey a person to the dingy precincts of hell rather than the gilded streets of heaven.

The shame of it all (and this may have been the way my child-like soul framed such events) is that I don't remember much of Jesus from them. That I remember these revivals as a source of trauma rather than grace is unfortunate. Because at the end of the day, it is the invitation of God's grace through Christ that will save us—not our fear of eternal damnation.

In retrospect, it seems ironic that we sang a song that celebrated God's love for me "just as I am" when the sermon of the hour had been about how God indeed doesn't accept me "just as I am." So, which is it? It can't be both! Either he does or he doesn't. I always had the feeling that I had to do something to make myself right with God before I could sing that song, which made no sense since the lyrics said I didn't need to do any such thing at all. Was I the only one who felt confused? I don't think so.

Today, I love that old hymn "Just as I Am." I see now how it reflects Christ's approach to the worst of the seven churches in the book of Revelation—one that was so far removed from its memory of Christ that it was threatened with expulsion from the kingdom (Rev 3:14–22). And yet it was to that same church among all of them that Christ said this: "Listen! I am standing at the door, knocking; if you hear my voice and open the door, I will come in to you and eat with you, and you with me" (v. 20).

While George Brunk II and others who thought we needed revival meetings were undoubtedly doing what they sensed God was asking of them (perhaps God was), it seems to me that we receive far more of "the fullness of God" in the spirit of Paul's prayer in Ephesians, a prayer I have found myself repeating a lot of late.

> For this reason I bow my knees before the Father, from whom every family in heaven and on earth takes its name. I pray that, according to the riches of his glory, he may grant that you may be strengthened in your inner being with power through his Spirit, and that Christ may dwell in your hearts

through faith, as you are being rooted and grounded in love. I pray that you may have the power to comprehend, with all the saints, what is the breadth and length and height and depth, and to know the love of Christ that surpasses knowledge, so that you may be filled with all the fullness of God. (Eph 3: 14–19)

CHAPTER ELEVEN

The End of 2020 and Still No Vaccine
May 2020

Everyone is racing to develop the first antidote for the novel coronavirus. We are told that a vaccine will be the key to ending this nightmare. Then we can all get back to school, back to baseball, back to barbershops and nail salons—back to normal. We are not the first, of course, to face a plague with no cure in sight.

The prophet Jeremiah bemoaned the fact that "the harvest is past, the summer has ended, and we are not saved" (Jer 8:20). From what exactly did God's good people need saving? Well, from venomous snakes that God sent slithering because of the sin of his people. And so the prophet grieved: "Is there no balm in Gilead? Is there no physician there? Why is there no healing for the wound of my people?" Or shall we say, we've gotten to the end of this plaguing pandemic year and still no vaccine, no balm?

A Facebook friend challenged my recent post as "blaming" God for this coronavirus mess, and instead made the case for God as the giver of life. About that essential life-giving characteristic of the Holy One, I have no doubt. Yet, in the same breath, it seems clear enough to me that we are pretty poor judges as to what truly makes for giving life and, conversely, bringing death—and, consequently, those aspects of life and death that are most damning to our souls.

While seemingly thinking aloud to himself about the gravity of the situation, God said to Jeremiah, "I will now refine and test them, for what else can I do with my sinful people?" (Jer 9:7). Like loving parents deeply grieved and regretting the need to discipline their children, God asked Jeremiah, "Have you seen what she did, that faithless one, Israel, how she went up on every hill and under every green tree, and played the whore there? And I thought, 'After she has done all this she will return to me'; but she did not return" (3:6–7a). So:

> Go, and proclaim these words toward [her], and say: Return, faithless Israel, says the Lord. I will not look on you in anger, for I am merciful . . . I will not be angry forever. Only acknowledge your guilt, that you have rebelled against the Lord your God . . . and have not obeyed my voice. (vv. 11–13)
>
> I thought how I would set you among my children, and give you a pleasant land, the most beautiful heritage of all the nations. And I thought you would call me, My Father, and would not turn from following me. Instead, . . . you have been faithless to me, O house of Israel. (vv. 19–20)

While reading this particular passage for the first time back in 2006, and feeling just a bit of the pain that God surely felt from the rejection of his people, I heard God mumbling, as it were, "My beloved children, I thought that once I gave you the *good life*, you would call me My Father!"

Sometimes we leave God with but little recourse except to jump in and scatter a few snakes in our path. Those snakes—their bites, if not their slithering—may keep us from pursuing a course of unholy damnation we are currently embarked upon, and deter us from the perils of hell toward which we are careening headlong. I don't know about you, but a snake in my path seems a lot more loving and far less threatening to my destiny than cascading over some self-inflicted precipice into unstoppable ruin—apart from the graciousness of God who would summon me back into his saving embrace, not later but now. Just so, it was due to a timely encounter with a lowly herd of swine that the prodigal son reversed course and came home to "My Father" whose waiting arms were wide open to receive him (Luke 15:1–24).

In the book of Numbers, it is recorded that God sent poisonous snakes in response to the complaint-and-blame-game that the Israelites had waged against God, having stirred it up in their Hebrew version of "Facebook" (aka the desert wilderness), where to face the direness of want and deprivation was to face their desperate need for God (Num 21:6–9).

Predictably, those desert people, being short on water and long on "this miserable food" that they continually harped about, eventually repented of their sin of faithlessness and pleaded with Moses to do something about those pesky little snakes slithering about! God's answer was to present them with yet another snake, one that he commanded Moses to fashion out of bronze and place upon a pole, so that "whenever a serpent bit someone, that person would look at the serpent of bronze and live" (vv. 8–9). Yes, *live!*

Moving forward to the New Testament, we find Jesus comparing himself with that same bronze wilderness snake: "Just as Moses lifted up the serpent in the desert, so the Son of Man must be lifted up, that everyone who believes in him may have eternal life" (John 3:14). Do we not see how amazing this is? At Golgotha, Jesus took upon himself the curse of the serpent to inflict sin and death, yet God's power raised Jesus up from death to life.

Folks, the reality is that the sting of death and the fatal virus of unredeemed sin are much more lethal than any novel coronavirus. So, while we may or may not have been vaccinated for Covid by the end of this year, the vaccine we most need for the deadliest of all viruses, our estrangement from God, has already arrived to heal, forgive, and restore us to life. Isaiah put it this way: "He was pierced for our transgressions, he was crushed for our iniquities; the punishment that brought us peace was on him, and by his wounds we are healed" (Isa 53:5–6).

As terrifying as it is to contemplate the imponderable mystery of that gruesome scene upon the crossbeams of Calvary, it is for us both virus and vaccine. "By his wounds we are healed."

CHAPTER TWELVE

A Third Great Awakening?
May 2020

With all the clamoring to get back to being in church these days, one would think we were in the midst of yet another Great Awakening in this country. Could it be that God must be greatly impressed with our urgent desire to return to our normal ways of worship?

Why, within the span of just two months, the very people who had given their pastors a hard time for asking them to come more often to church are now the same people beating up on their pastors for saying it's a bit too early to open the church's doors. Those who formerly found every excuse in the book to do something other than go to church on Sunday are suddenly about to burst through the ramparts even if, thanks to Covid, doing so might cost them their lives in the process. What an impressive display of sudden zeal and commitment for the faith during these pandemic days in America— "taking a stand for God," they call it!

The problem is that this race toward the sanctuary is awfully reminiscent of what Jeremiah faced in the sixth century B.C., when the people poured through the gates of the temple crying, "This is the temple of the Lord, the temple of the Lord, the temple of the Lord!" (Jer 7:4). But neither Jeremiah nor God was impressed by their zealous piety, because nothing had changed with their behavior.

Thus says the Lord God of hosts, the God of Israel: Amend your ways and your doings, and let me dwell with you in this place. . . . For if you truly amend your ways and your doings, if you truly act justly one with another, if you do not oppress the alien, the orphan, and the widow, or shed innocent blood in this place, and if you do not go after other gods to your own hurt, then I will dwell with you in this place. . . . Here you are, trusting in deceptive words to no avail. Will you . . . come and stand before me in this house, which is called by my name, and say, 'We are safe!'—only to go on doing these abominations?" (7:3b–10)

It is not surprising to me, then, that the number of folks who "liked" my Facebook post about our country's historic sins of racism paled in comparison to those who "liked" everything else I've written. Why so? Because it's risky business to point out our country's deep structural sin of disregard for the poor, the alien, the fatherless, the widow, and those whom this nation has oppressed because of the color of their skin.

For a nation that historically has prided itself in being a shining beacon on a hill, the national light has shown pretty dimly of late. All the more dreadful is when the church falls prey to the politics of the day and fails to shine God's greater light upon the darkness of the principalities and powers that oppress "the alien, the orphan, and the widow" whom it is God's practice to embrace and defend.

So, when you or I lament that "I can't wait to get back to church," the question we may need to raise is this: Have I taken the time during these several months of quarantine to reset my life in such a way as to show my concern for the poor, the immigrant, and the fatherless more so than I did before the onset of Covid? I can't answer that question for you or anyone else. Yet, for myself I know that when I take the Lord's words at face value—to "be still and know that I am God"—then I allow God's Spirit to do the deep heart-work of breaking through to me, knowing that I am still far from where I need to be.

Do you think that God would be more impressed with a new-found compassion for the poor, the alien, and the destitute than with clamoring to get back to the church? There is always the chance that we might throng through the doors of our temple buildings next Sunday, leaving Jesus outside ministering to those we pass by in a hurry to return to the place where we believe, like the Israelites, "we are safe!" Yet, as for the many who do not have any earthly safety or sanctuary to call their own, do you think they might come clamoring at our doors on a Sunday or any other day of the week, expecting to find safety and sanctuary in the light and love of Jesus whom they see in our faces?

A Third Great Awakening is possible. But as in Jeremiah's day it requires more than a deep wish to get back to the temple. In case we may have lost sight of it, and if there be any "getting back," it would be to the practice of an awakened religion of the heart. Because such a religion exists not for itself but for the world that God "so loved" and continues to love—including and especially the world of the alien, the fatherless, the widow, and the multitude for whom Jesus multiplied the loaves and the fishes (Luke 9:10–17).

We read in the Gospel of Luke that upon seeing the five thousand who had followed Jesus to Bethsaida as the day drew to a close, the twelve disciples said to Jesus: "Send the crowd away, so that they may go into the surrounding villages and countryside, to lodge and get provisions; for we are here in a deserted place. But he said to them, 'You give them something to eat'. . . . And taking the five loaves and the two fish, he looked up into heaven and blessed and broke them, and gave them to the disciples to set before the crowd. And all ate and were filled" (vv. 12b–17a).

It was a day of great awakening in Bethsaida. For the place to which the disciples had withdrawn "privately" with Jesus was no longer "a deserted place." Luke the evangelist had delivered a clear message to his readers about the mission of Christ's people in all places.

CHAPTER THIRTEEN

Nobody Asks, "Where Is the Lord?"
May 2020

During the global pandemic, I read a Facebook post from some-one whose ninety-seven-year old grandmother survived Covid and was released from the hospital. Rather than giving thanks to God, this self-proclaimed follower of Jesus railed against the state of Pennsylvania's governor and its secretary of health, blaming them for his grandmother's illness.

Then again, I was recently in a meeting of folks who were concerned about their employment status going forward. When they learned that their jobs were intact for now, they responded not with gratitude and humility but with a spirit of entitlement and hubris, accusing their employers of taking advantage of them in a time of crisis. Why so? Because apparently someone must be blameworthy for our crisis-induced pain.

Someone like President Donald Trump, China, Nancy Pelosi, state governors, Amazon, former President Barak Obama, Dr. Fauci, Dr. Birx, former Vice President Joe Biden, people wearing masks, people not wearing masks, the media on the left, the media on the right, the media not knowing where it is. And where does this list of the blameworthy end? Everyone is to blame, that is, everyone except for "me." Because if "I" were to blame, then "I" would need to do something besides blab on Facebook about "my" displeasure with everyone else.

Why are we so busy blaming humans that we cannot fathom the possibility that God may have something personally to do with this worldwide pandemic? Why doesn't God's name come to the surface more often during the blame-game? Why isn't at least every other person who's shuffling along Main Street placing ultimate responsibility at God's feet for the big mess we're in? Is it because we can't believe that a loving God could be implicated in such universal suffering? And is it because we have come to believe that God has so little to do with human affairs that we don't bother to ask anymore, "Where is the Lord?"

We preachers and pew-dwellers alike, have we abandoned the thought (or is it the conviction?) that the Creator-Redeemer-God stands above, beneath, behind, and deep within this present pandemic? In fact, might it be that God is the very one who is disrupting the customary ways of our living and dying by plaguing us with this wretched coronavirus? Perish the conviction, we say. Most of us cringe at the thought.

But then, God said to Moses who declared to Egypt's Pharoah: "Thus says the Lord, 'By this you shall know that I am the Lord.' See, with the staff that is in my hand I will strike the water that is in the Nile, and it shall be turned to blood" (Exod 7:17). "I will plague your whole country with frogs," and "gnats," and "flies," and "deadly pestilence" to "livestock," with "festering boils on humans and animals," with "thunder and hail, and fire," with "locusts," and "'darkness over the land of Egypt, a darkness that can be felt'" (chs. 8–10, passim).

> "Thus says the Lord: About midnight I will go out through Egypt. Every firstborn in the land of Egypt shall die, from the firstborn of Pharoah who sits on his throne to the firstborn of the female slave who is behind the handmill, and all the firstborn of the livestock. Then there will be a loud cry throughout the whole land of Egypt, such as has never been or will ever be again." (11:4–6)

So, what about today? Is a plague by the hand of God too much for us to countenance? Is a pandemic by the hand of God too much for us to conceive of because it is beyond belief, beyond reason, beyond counting, controlling, and predicting? Or, is our God simply a clock-maker God far too removed from it all to be intricately involved in the upheavals of human history, a God who long since has vanished from the scene and left the clock to tick all on its own, come willy-nilly what may? So, let's ask ourselves again. Is it true that we have come to believe that God has so little to do with human affairs that we don't bother to ask anymore, "Where is the Lord?"

In the prophet Jeremiah's day, according to the book that bears his name, God was grievously disgruntled. Why do we suppose? It was because the Israelites did not bother to ask that very same question, "Where is the Lord?" Not once, but twice, "They did not say, 'Where is the Lord?'"

> Thus says the Lord: What wrong did your ancestors find in me that they went far from me, and . . . did not say, "Where is the Lord who brought us up from the land of Egypt, who led us in the wilderness, in a land of deserts and pits, in a land of drought and deep darkness, in a land that no one passes through, where no one lives?" (Jer 2:6)

Moreover, "the priests did not say, 'Where is the Lord?'" (v. 8a). But you'd think that the Israelites, and especially their priests, would have been asking that question, wouldn't you? And if not when things were all hunky-dory, then at least when things went south, or, in Jeremiah's case, north. For the Jerusalemites were being hauled off to the north into exile in Babylon, thanks to King Nebuchadnezzar. So you would think that by now they would be asking, "Where is the Lord?"

So, ponder this: Jeremiah declares that God is the one enlisting Nebuchadnezzar's army to do the hauling away. For it is God who is the one calling the shots from behind the scene.

> For thus says the Lord to the people . . . Declare in Judah, and proclaim in Jerusalem, and say: Blow the trumpet through the land; shout aloud and say, "Gather together. . . ." Raise a standard toward Zion, flee for safety, do not delay, for I am bringing evil from the north, and a great destruction. A lion has gone up from its thicket, a destroyer of nations has set out; he has gone out from his place to make your land a waste; your cities will be ruins without inhabitant. Because of this put on sackcloth, lament and wail: "The fierce anger of the Lord has not turned away from us." (4:3–8)

This destruction is God's doing! For the Israelites "have perverted their way, they have forgotten the Lord their God" (3:21b).

> O Jerusalem. . . . "Besiegers come from a distant land; they shout against the cities of Judah. They have closed in around her like watchers of a field, because she has rebelled against me, says the Lord. Your ways and your doings have brought this upon you. This is your doom; how bitter it is! It has reached your very heart." (4:14–18)

How bitter it is, friends. How bitter it is to endure the Lord's judgment. Can our ears bear asking, "Where is the Lord?" amid this worldwide coronavirus? Is it God's "dismantling"? Is it God's judging of the people of the earth for having "forgotten the Lord their God"? Is it God's doing?—and our undoing?—by God's hand?

"But, wait a minute!" you say. "Conrad, that's Old Testament stuff. The New Testament God is a different God." But is that so?

How often, if but too often, has the Christian church in the course of its history toyed with the scam put forth in the second century AD, by the wealthy shipowner and heretic Marcion, who went all about the Mediterranean claiming that the God of the New Testament was a different God than the God of the Old? So different a God that Marcion sought to banish the Hebrew scriptures altogether, in favor of a God whose love knew neither law nor judgment. But the Orthodox churches would have none of it. They said unmistakably to Marcion: You've got it wrong. There is only one God of the Old and the New, of the Jew and the Christian, whose gospel of faithful love is inclusive of both law and judgment.

In the year 2020, here is what is at issue, as I see it: Are we prepared to embrace the God who is the God of both Jeremiah and Jesus, of Isaiah and John? The God who lives at the very center of the universe as its creator, judge, and redeemer? The God who through Jeremiah declares, "For if you truly amend your ways and your doings, if you truly act justly one with another, if you do not oppress the alien, the orphan, and the widow, or shed innocent blood in this place, and if you do not go after other gods to your own hurt, then I will dwell with you in this place" (Jer 7:5–7)?

The God who speaks to us through Jesus in the Gospel of John declares, "If you believed Moses, you would believe me, for he wrote about me. But if you do not believe what he wrote, how will you believe what I say?" (John 5:46–47). It was this same God who declared through Isaiah, "In the wilderness prepare the way of the Lord, make straight in the desert a highway for our God" (Isa 40:3). And the apostle John, envisioning a new heaven and a new earth, pictures God seated on the throne, saying, "'See, I am making all things new.' Also saying, 'Write this, for these words are trustworthy and true'" (Rev. 21:5).

So, let's come back to our original question, "Where is the Lord?" Where is the Lord in the midst of this Covid pandemic? By God's hand, what is God doing, and undoing, through this viral plague? As best I know how, I can answer only by speaking very personally.

Some time ago, without bitterness or resentment, I heard myself saying, "When God gave me Parkinson's disease . . ." I realized in that particular moment that I had come to a point in the course of this unwanted "dis-ease," of placing it, of placing my life, within God's story and God's hands. I lovingly attributed Parkinson's to being more about God than about me. I did so because I had come to trust that God, to this very day, is up to an ultimate good in my life even though I cannot fully comprehend it.

Which leads me finally to these words of the apostle John: "'See, the home of God is among mortals. He will dwell with them as their God; they will be as his peoples, and God himself will be with them; he will wipe away every tear from their eyes. Death will be no more; mourning and crying and pain will be no more, for the first things have passed away'" (Rev 21:3b–4; see Ezek 37:27 and Isa 25:8, 35:10).

This too, my friends, shall be by God's hand.

CHAPTER FOURTEEN

Racism: Sin Then—the Same Sin Now
May 2020

The Covid pandemic of 2020 has revealed what many have known and expressed. If you are a person of black or brown skin you are more likely to die from the disease earlier in life than those of white skin. If you are African-American or Latino you are more likely than White people to contract and succumb to the coronavirus.

Of course, the disparities would have nothing to do with the color of one's skin or the place of one's birth, that is, except for the fact that nearly three hundred years ago our nation's founding fathers, aligned as they were with the scientific principles and methods of their day, were quite content to uphold a social construct that was deeply entrenched in racial inequities.

Thomas Jefferson, well known for the Jefferson Bible from which he removed all texts containing the miracles of Jesus, hypothesized that persons possessing dark skin were less intelligent, and thereby lesser humans than persons of light skin.[9]

Jefferson's subjective theory of racial inequality lent credence to the emergence of "race science" or, more precisely, "scientific racism" as espoused by movers and shakers of the dominant European-American social, academic, philanthropic, and political culture.

---

[9]   See Thomas Jefferson, *Notes on the State of Virginia*, Query XIV, "Laws," beginning with "To emancipate all slaves born after passing the act . . ." https://avalon.law.yale.edu/18th_century/jeffvir.asp/.

America's original sin of racism, already rooted in European-ized colonialization and institutionalized chattel slavery a century and a half before the nation's founding, eventuated in the widespread twentieth-century practice of eugenics. Eugenics in the United States involved the forced sterilizations of thousands of Blacks, Native Americans, the mentally ill, and close to a third of Puerto Rican women. The movement extended beyond our borders to Great Britain, France, and Germany, and in the latter instance became a major inspiration for the Third Reich's demonic experimentation with racial cleansing aimed at eradicating the Jews and others deemed social misfits, for the sake of purifying the Aryan race.

In an ironic footnote to Germany's collective racism, where Black athletes were considered inferior to their White counterparts, the African-American track and field star, Jesse Owens, made a fool of Hitler's "race science" right beneath Hitler's nose. Mr. Owens became the celebrated four-time gold medalist of Berlin's 1936 summer Olympics. As a result of his indubitable prowess, "race scientists" began to change their tune to say that Blacks' physiological superiority was due to their being "closer to the primitive"—a classic instance of rationalizing racist postulations in order to maintain the myth of White supremacy while at the same time accounting for Mr. Owens's irrefutable triumph.

It was all the more ironic that Mr. Owens, the grandson of Southern slaves, returned home from the plaudits of cheering crowds in Nazi Germany, only to be subjected to the degrading indignities of Jim Crow segregation. After a hero's parade in New York City, he proceeded to a reception held in his honor at the Waldorf Astoria Hotel. There he was required to take the service elevator instead of the one reserved for guests. President Franklin Roosevelt failed to offer congratulations. Southern newspapers refused to publish photos of Mr. Owens's Olympian achievement.

Subsequent to the flattery of raining tickertape, the black-skinned gold medalist went to work as a janitor in a children's playground and as a service station attendant pumping gas. "After I came home from the 1936 Olympics with my four medals," he said, "it became increasingly apparent that everyone was going to slap me on the back, want to shake my hand, or have me up to their suite. But no one was going to offer me a job." "I had four gold medals, but you can't eat four gold medals."[10]

Beyond the flagrant discriminations of Jim Crow segregation and the shameless mob lynchings of Blacks, racial inequities and systemic injustices have persisted in our own time for African-Americans. The rash of killings of Black citizens by White police officers, for one. The mass incarceration of young Blacks by White-led judicial systems, for two. The decimation of Black neighborhoods by creeping White gentrification, for three. The disparity between the payments of Black wages and White wages, for four. And today, the high rate of Black deaths relative to White deaths due to Covid. And that's not all, for the long shadow of slavery as America's original sin hangs over the entire American landscape like a giant pall.

So, to what then does this sordid history of White racism and White supremacy beckon us Christians now?

As Evangelicals, lest we forget, scripture summons us to the removal of blinders with respect to the collective sin of wholesale domination that invariably leads to the evils of social, political, and economic enslavement. Remember, it was our spiritual ancestors who were enslaved in Egypt. For that reason, the Mosaic law specifically says, "You shall not wrong or oppress a resident alien; you know the heart of an alien, for you were aliens in the land of Egypt" (Exod 23:9). "The alien who resides with you shall be to you as the citizen

---

[10]   https://www.biography.com/news/jesse-owens-biography-olympic-triumphs-olympic-sized-struggles-20892201/.

among you; you shall love the alien as yourself, for you were aliens in the land of Egypt: I am the Lord your God" (Lev 19:34).

Were that text to be written for us White European-Americans today, it would read: You shall love the immigrant as yourself, for you were once immigrants—aliens—yourselves!

Was that not also true for Africans as they first set foot on the shores of Virginia, the Carolinas, and Georgia, having endured the throes of hell as human cargo chained to the blood-stained holds of slave ships during the Middle Passage through the waters of the Atlantic? Was it not the case that those dark-skinned women, men, and children of God were branded as resident aliens the minute they touched their toes on the White Man's turf which the White Man had seized from the Native American? Was it not tragic, beyond belief, that Whites sought to strip Blacks of the divinely given dignity and worth of their very humanity?

By the crack of the whip and the dangling of the noose, entire populations of our White "Christian" forebears coerced African bodies, minds, and spirits to bend over row-after-row of cotton bolls and tobacco leaves, day-in-and-day-out, year-after-year, in sweltering toil beneath the baking sun. To what end? So that the oppression of the Black Man would assure the economic prosperity and political hegemony of the White Man. Sadly, prosperity deafens and hegemony blinds.

Did our White ancestors not read from the same Bible as we modern Evangelicals do? Yet, because prosperity deafens and hegemony blinds, whenever our White forebears spuriously and selectively dipped into their Bibles to find validation for a system of oppression that required obedience of slaves to their masters, they turned a deaf ear and blind eye to God's commandments: "You shall not wrong or oppress a resident alien" (Exod 22:21). "You shall love the alien as yourself" (Lev 19:34b).

There is no shortage of scripture that summons us as God's people to the confession of our sin.

> The Lord spoke to Moses, saying: Speak to the Israelites: When a man or a woman wrongs another, breaking faith with the Lord, that person incurs guilt and shall confess the sin that has been committed. The person shall make full restitution for the wrong, adding one fifth to it, and giving it to the one who was wronged. (Num 5:5–7)
>
> Then those of Israelite descent . . . stood and confessed their sins and the iniquities of their ancestors. They stood up in their place and read from the book of the law of the Lord their God for a fourth part of the day, and for another fourth they made confession and worshipped the Lord their God. (Neh 9:2–3)

The authenticity of our confession and the validity of our worship reveal our love for God to the extent of our love for "the least of these" among us. Jesus's words, spoken through the Gospel of Matthew, make this abundantly clear.

> "When the Son of Man comes in his glory, and all the angels with him, then he will sit on the throne of his glory. All the nations will be gathered before him, and he will separate people one from another as a shepherd separates the sheep from the goats, he will put the sheep at his right hand and the goats at the left." (Matt 25:31–33)

Our ancestors knew, and we know, the rest of that story. It's entirely too memorable to be forgotten, far too important to be ignored. Jesus will not be asking whether we are Christians or non-Christians, Protestants or Catholics, Mainliners or Evangelicals,

Mennonites or Baptists. Rather, he will judge how we measured up to the following:

> "I was hungry and you gave me food, I was thirsty and you gave me something to drink. I was a stranger and you welcomed me, I was naked and you gave me clothing, I was sick and you took care of me, I was in prison and you visited me . . . 'Truly I tell you, just as you did it to one of the least of these who are members of my family, you did it to me.'" (vv. 35–36, 40)

CHAPTER FIFTEEN

If Truth Sets Us Free—Why Do We Hear So Little of It in Church?
May 2020

I've been reading Erik Larson's excellent book, *The Splendid and the Vile*, a biography of Winston Churchill as he confronted Germany's seemingly unstoppable march across Europe during the Second World War. Despite his many flaws as a human being, yet no more flawed than the rest of us, Churchill told the truth. He leveled with his fellow Brits. He told them that their chances of surviving Hitler's assault were slim, but he declared: "We shall defend our island, whatever the cost may be, we shall fight on the beaches, we shall fight on the landing grounds, we shall fight in the fields and in the streets, we shall fight in the hills; we shall never surrender."[11]

When I was thirty-five years old, I was diagnosed with papillary thyroid cancer, a battle that lasted three years and included multiple surgeries and nearly a lifetime's dose of radiation. But I remember in those moments, despite the terror that awakened me most mornings, that I simply wanted to know the truth. "Doctor, don't beat around the bush, don't play games, don't sugarcoat—just tell me what you see." I wanted to know the truth, for knowing the truth would free me to live the life I wanted to live, even if it be brief.

It was also during those terror-stricken mornings that I began to go deeper with God, awakening early to spend time listening for

---

[11]   Erik Larson, *The Splendid and the Vile: A Saga of Churchill, Family, and Defiance During the Blitz* (New York: Crown, 2020), 58.

God to speak his truth, and for me to find comfort and courage in words the Holy Spirit had inspired saints to write across the centuries. For if the Bible is worth anything at all, it's because it speaks truth, including truths not found elsewhere. The holy scriptures don't sugarcoat, don't deny, and don't cover up.

We can quibble all we want about historic manuscripts, verbal inconsistencies, and who wrote just what, all of which quibbling has become little more than meaningless babble to me. These arguments too often are for folks who aren't enlisted on the front-lines of battle. Theirs is the luxury of extended "time-out" for debate.

What I know when I read the scriptures is that I'm hearing the truth about how bad things really are on the battlefield. And I'm also hearing about how we're going to get out of this big mess we're in, one way or another. I know this not because someone told me that the Bible speaks truth and therefore is true. I know this because over the decades of crisis after crisis the words of its truth have always shown up in time to be true to my life. What you need when you've been shot in battle is not a lecture on the history of medicine. What you need is a medic.

During my first year of thyroid cancer, I consulted an endocrinologist who was legally blind. When results from the second year's bloodwork pointed to a recurrence of the disease, he acknowledged having read the laboratory report, but he said he couldn't see where on the films the disease was located. Dissatisfied with not knowing the truth, I transferred to another hospital and to a particular physician who, as he looked at the film, said, "Why, right here it is," to my great relief. Surgery followed, with more radiation. If I hadn't known the truth, due to the simple fact that someone had actually seen and spoken the truth, I wouldn't have known at that point what to do.

One reason I continue to love the Bible is that it never diminishes the current difficulty in which I find myself. At the same time, the Bible validates a greater truth than the present difficulty itself. The scriptures point me, with hope, beyond the momentary truth of my situation to the greater truth of God's providence—of which the root word is "provide." It's the difference between seeing but a single lonely lost star in the night sky and gazing in contrast upon the vast darkness lit up by a magnificent canopy of twinkling stars.

I am not alone in my travail. You are not alone in yours. As with Churchill speaking truthfully to the British people with honest and determined hope, we need not surrender in the midst of our distress.

Within and beyond every current crisis, a cosmic story is being written by the hand of God—a monumental story, which is the story the church is given to tell. To tell as the storm clouds gather. To tell as the darkness descends. To tell until the nocturnal moon gives way to the morning sunrise. Why? Because "God so loved the world." Because God-in-Christ came "not to condemn the world, but that the world might be saved" (John 3:16a,17b, RSV). This is God's business, always God's business, giving life and saving life.

I grew up in a culture that put a lot of emphasis on looking good and doing everything right, but overlooked the truth about what was actually going on inside of me and within the church itself. The problem for me was that I never felt I was getting it right or measuring up. As a child this tormented me and kept me awake at night. The incongruity between what I was told I should be and what I knew of myself, as I really was, nearly drove me insane. As a result, I've often wondered why in the world I stuck it out with any affirmative sense of God. For the life of me, I couldn't figure out for a long time how I could ever speak to others of "good news" when the news I was hearing never felt good at all. The last thing I wanted was to project upon the church my own inner torment.

Somehow the truth about the mess I'd come to think of myself as being in, and the truth of God's incredible love for me as the answer to that mess, never came together. And that was despite more Sundays spent in church listening to sermons and singing hymns than I could begin to count. It was only when I was in my early twenties, as my life fell apart and everyone could see me for the broken person I was, that I finally encountered the indispensable truth I'd been missing all along.

What was that truth? Very simply, that "God so loved me." And not because I "grew up in church." Not because I knew how to "dress up for church." Not because I was "good enough for church." And not even because I was "Christian." But solely because God had created me and placed upon and within me his everlasting imprint of worth and goodness.

I also had the realization that this is the spot-on truth for every single person in the world, no matter how messed up people might be. We are each one a child of God. Some may not yet know it. Others may be clinging to their doubt and uncertainty. And, yes, as C.S. Lewis said, even if offered the gift of Childhood while staring over the precipice of Hades, some would still reject it. But that would not be because God willed it so.

I've spent a lot of time with Millennials and Generation X-ers and Y-ers—the folks who are exiting the church most rapidly these days. I've come to love them as friends and feel more comfortable with them than I often do with church people, in large part because they recognize how messed up they are and we all are. They are honest. They openly talk about their problems. They share their mental health diagnoses. They express their doubts and fears. They cry. They confess. And I'm finding that I love their honesty because it is a context in which I am able to be honest with them too. In admitting their messes, they accept me with mine. And every now and then, one of them approaches me to ask about the hope that is within me. That's "Hope" with a capital "H," which also stands for "Holy."

Yes, this group has had difficulty accepting my invitation to "come to church." But I think I've begun to understand why. It's because wherever personal truths are neither told nor received with acceptance, Grand Truth seems irrelevant and devoid of meaning. So, whenever you and I find ourselves "going back to church" post-Covid, I hope we return to telling our truths, and to telling Truth with a capital "T." We may just discover that some of our non-churched friends will also show up for the telling, because what they want, and we want, truthfully, is authenticity. God is forever in the business of truth-telling, both God's and ours.

The truth that God is love. The truth that we are loved. For this is the cosmic story we all want to hear, especially on a cloudy day.

CHAPTER SIXTEEN

When God Disappeared
From the Church?
June 2020

No one is exactly sure when God disappeared from the church, if in fact it was so, as reported by some.

Today's sociologists possess no sure-fire metrics by which to measure the whereabouts of God, much less to resolve any lingering doubts about the Almighty's very existence. Even if they could, few of us would take them at their word. However, the Big Three theorists of the sociological enterprise of more than a century ago were fixated upon the subject of God, or at least the subject of religion.

Karl Marx, for one, said that God was a drug to keep the religious masses "pacified." To the limited extent that he was able to focus his observation upon the nineteenth-century European masses, he may have concluded more or less correctly, about those "drugged" aspects of acculturated Christianity, or more accurately that they should be labeled as "passified." Note the difference in spelling of the words. *Passive* is different from *pacific*, for the former denotes acquiescence and the latter peacefulness.

Had Marx looked in greater detail farther west, the glaring exception would have been the anything-but-passive Christianity practiced by African-Americans. For them, God was and is, not an acquiescent God but an active and engaging God, a living presence to be reckoned with on a daily basis.

Just so, African-American religion provided its adherents a constant source of nurturance and hope throughout the interminable horrors of slavery. And African-American Christianity remains today a plain-spoken, demonstrative faith in the God in whom, as Saint Paul put it, we all "live and move and have our being" (Acts 17:28a). It was the vibrant Christianity of African-Americans that electrified the twentieth century's Civil Rights Movement and inspired their refusal to take their seats at the back of the bus.

> Have you got good religion? Certainly, Lord!
> Have you got good religion? Certainly, Lord!
> Have you got good religion? Certainly, Lord!
> Cer-t'nly, Cer-t'nly, Cer-t'nly, Lord![12]

Contrast the effusive call-and-response of that old Negro spiritual with the fact that the sociologist Émile Durkheim, the patriarch of modern social science, when writing from France, argued that while religion was good for creating shared moral values, the church was simply a group of folks who hung out together, mostly worshipping themselves.

The German theorist Max Weber, on the other hand, challenged empirically reductionist explanations of complex social realities and promoted instead the idea that the modern world—caught up in its iron cage of rationality, of counting things, controlling things, predicting things, and doing all things with numbing efficiency—would only be rescued from its imprisonment by charismatic prophets and reimagined ancient ideas.

Of all social institutions that might have an inkling of a rightful claim to age-old charismatic prophesies and neglected words of the wise, it's the synagogue and the church that possess the longest

---

[12]   "Certainly, Lord," traditional Negro spiritual.

history of having evoked such curiosities whenever God gave them timely birth. Just as African-American prophetic Christianity arose out of backwoods praise houses amid the cruel and oppressive ethos of an enslaved and segregated South, so too does a faithful church today possess Pentecostal powers with which to "stand against the wiles of the devil . . . against the rulers, against the authorities, against the cosmic powers of this present darkness," yes, and even "against the spiritual forces of evil in the heavenly places" (Eph 6:11b–12). For those divine powers are around, about, below, above, and beyond all earthly principalities and powers.

> When Israel was in E-gypt's land: Let my peo-ple go;
> Op-pressed so hard they could not stand, Let my people go.
> Go down, Mo-ses, 'Way down in E-gypt land,
> Tell ole Pharaoh, Let my peo-ple go.[13]

Theologians and prophets and apostles of the church, please. Please come forward. Please come forth and help us to reimagine and claim those ancient prophetic powers. Please don't get so mired down in the muck of getting tenured and published and promoted that you have nothing to say "in print" or "out of print." Most of all, in your "living voice" do not fail to enthuse the minds and warm the hearts of saints who tomorrow morning and afternoon will require Pentecostal powers with which to carry on. For, just as it was true generations ago, they will need those ancient words and wisdom-refrains to confront "ole Pharoah 'Way down in E-gypt land." And why? Because Pharoah, he's still hangin' around, waitin' for a come-back.

While I suspect that most theologians and pastors likely still believe in God, they also know that "church" can take place without God most Sundays. But then they recognize that it won't be church if it is

---

[13]   "Go Down, Moses," traditional Negro spiritual.

without God. And they know that most of today's worldly saints can make out just fine from Monday through Saturday without having had a world-shattering encounter with God, whether on Sunday or any other day of the week. And that's because a saint's comfort level can remain reasonably comfortable so long as God doesn't trouble it much.

What's most tragic is when God's knock upon the church door is hammer-heavy deafening, but from within the church no one hears anything that would arouse so much as a common housefly, and mostly because the folks on the inside of the church, including and especially the preacher, may have forgotten that worship, like prayer, begins and ends with deep listening.

If conscientious prayer, inside or outside the church (and academy), is hard to come by, then, quite simply, pause wherever you are. Begin first by closing your eyes. And then say in the long silence, "Dear God, I'm listening." Or say, "Father of Mercies and Mother of Love, be present to me in the midst of my morning mess and my evening distress. I'm listening."

Or say, "Holy Spirit, will you, please? Please show up because my mama's fast dying in the hospital of Covid, but I can't reach my arms through the window to throw them around her." Then, once you've pled your prayer, go ahead and cry your tears. Because your crying is as good as your listening when you've run out of everything to say to God.

What must the God of the Bible do more than he's already done to show us that he comes to us, and that in coming to us he loves us, and that in loving us he does not forsake us? Is this not true whether we've already come to him begging, or not? How do you come, anyway, to somebody who's already beside you? By opening your eyes, your ears, and your heart. Because it's only his coming to you that makes possible your coming to him, whether in church or out of church, whether up one side of the mountain or down the other.

Think about it a minute. We ask God to come to our Sunday prayer gatherings. But then if nothing exciting, entertaining, or mind-blowing occurs, then we say something like, "Well, God just didn't show up today." If so, then perhaps it's because the prayer-professionals programmed spontaneity out of the service by requiring God and everyone else to stick to the printed order of worship in the bulletin. And in that case, we simply beat the drums and strum the guitars all the louder! But will our drumming and plucking the strings call forth holy smoke from the heavens?

Or, secretly, we feel like we have to bribe God to finally get his attention. So we bargain with the Holy One, and say, "If you will, then I will . . ." But then, what if the Holy One doesn't bargain with us? What if he simply lays it out there—grace, that is—and says, take it or leave it.

The late Elie Wiesel, a deeply devout Jew, one of the spiritual giants of our time, as a teenager was swept by the Nazis, along with Elie's family, from their home in Transylvania and transported to the concentration camp at Auschwitz. In his memoir entitled *Night*, he recounted the horrors of witnessing his mother, sister, and others in the family vanish into the abyss of Hitler's fiery furnaces.

Bunked in a barrack, subsisting on meager morsels of bread and water in painfully close quarters with fellow prisoners of the Holocaust, he and his father together witnessed inconceivable fear, suffering, and death first-hand, and corpses lying all over the place. "Evenings," he said, "as we lay on our cots, we sometimes tried to sing a few Hasidic melodies. . . . Some of the men spoke of God. . . . As for me, I had ceased to pray. I concurred with Job! I was not denying His existence, but I doubted His absolute justice."[14]

---

[14]   Elie Wiesel, *Night* (New York: Hill and Wang, Division of Farrar, Straus and Giroux, 1958), 45. The book won the Nobel Peace Prize.

Soon Elie and his father were transferred to another camp named Buna, and subsequently via a hellish journey by boxcar to the infamous Buchenwald where Elie watched his father's slow, cruel demise and death from starvation and dysentery. At one point while imprisoned in Buna, Elie witnessed a public hanging of three inmates who had been brought in chains to the "three gallows, three black ravens, erected on the Appelplatz," meaning the "place" of the "roll call." One of those three was a beautiful young child Elie named the "little . . . sad-eyed angel."[15]

"All eyes were on the child. He was pale, almost calm, but he was biting his lips as he stood in the shadow of the gallows."[16] The other two, about to be executed, shouted as the executioner hung nooses around all three necks. Yet the little boy remained silent.

Elie suddenly heard from behind him a voice asking, "Where is the merciful God, where is He?" And with that, the three chairs tipped over and the nooses tightened. Tears flowed as the crowd fell into dead silence and slowly processed past the victims. The two men died instantly, but the child, being of light weight, continued breathing "for more than half an hour, lingering between life and death, writhing before our eyes. . . He was still alive when I passed him," Elie said.

"Behind me, I heard the same man asking: 'For God's sake, where is God?' And from within me, I heard a voice answer: 'Where He is? This is where—hanging here from this gallows.'"[17]

It's true, isn't it? Sociologists, philosophers, pop-theologians, and misguided prophets possess no sure-fire metrics by which to measure the whereabouts of God. Yet, we must ask, is it also true that the church behind closed doors is sometimes nothing more than

---

[15]   *Night*, 64.
[16]   *Night*, 64.
[17]   *Night*, 65.

a group of folks who hang out together, mostly worshipping themselves? That certainly can't be true of God's synagogue and church huddled together in the blight and defacement of a concentration camp.

Maybe there's something extraordinary and for the most part invisible always going on here—something far more profound than sociologists, philosophers, pop-theologians, misguided prophets, media moguls, politicians, and the "good people" walking aimlessly down Main Street, who think they have no special need of God—something it's easy to be deaf and blind to—*Someone*, in fact, who's right here squarely in front of you each step of the way, suffering with you however you suffer, rejoicing with you however you rejoice, all the while walking beside you—the God who in Jesus Christ and in the "sad-eyed angel," *crucified*, is resurrected from the dead, incarnate, *alive* within you and among you, here and now!

"*Sure-ly been 'buked, and sure-ly been scorned,*" goes the old Negro spiritual.

"*No more auction block for me, No more, No more; No more driver's lash for me; No more, No more.*"

"*My Good Lord's done been here.*"

"*Oh, walk together, children, don't you get weary; Going to mourn and never tire; sing and never tire; pray and never tire; shout and never tire; Oh, I feel the spirit moving; For Jesus is a-coming. There's a great camp-meeting in the Promised Land.*"

"*He made the sun to shine by day, He made the sun to show the way; His love an' pow-er will pre-vail, His prom-is-es will nev-er fail; God is a God An' He al-ways will be God!*"[18]

---

[18]   Lines from traditional Negro spirituals, in successive order, "Free at Last," "Many Thousand Gone," "My Good Lord's Done Been Here," "There's a Great Camp Meeting," "God Is a God."

Yes, Crucifixion Day is now Resurrection Day and Pentecost Day all rolled into One. So, when you ask, "Has God disappeared from the church?" the answer is, "Of course not!"

Not from those horrific concentration camps. Not from those early praise houses where Black slaves found the sure hope to believe that their Exodus was just around the corner. Not even from where you sit reading.

"Where is the Lord?" You know the answer. He is *here*. He is *there*. He is *everywhere*.

PART FOUR

GOOD NEWS FOR A CHURCH DISMANTLED

CHAPTER SEVENTEEN

A Block Party Hymn Sing—
Not in My Backyard!
May 2020

So Jeremiah gives God's people the good news that they are to settle down in Babylon among their enemies, have children, see them get married, plant gardens and, by the way, "seek the welfare of the city where I have sent you into exile, and pray to the Lord on its behalf, for in its welfare you will find your welfare" (Jer 29:7).

These two directives seem so confoundedly contradictory. The exiles are to hunker down among their enemies and yet remain faithful to Yahweh and the Torah. And all the while they must pray for and rub shoulders with those pagan neighbors who are their worst nightmare.

You see, from the outset, the purposes of God were never intended to be solely for the Hebrew covenant people nor only for those Gentiles who became followers of Jesus. For in both the Old and New Testaments the kingdom of God flies overhead, in front of, and beyond the nation of Israel and the Christian church. Neither is an end in and of itself. Both Israel and the church are to be subject to the flowering of God's kingdom, which is not restricted by the law of gravity any more than it is by the gravity of any particular moment in history. And yet the situation for the Jerusalemites in Babylon is grave.

So, how well do God's people do with this pray-for-the-prosperity-of-Babylon thing? Lest their experience be lost on us, Psalm 137 gives clear clues.

"By the rivers of Babylon—there we sat down and there we wept when we remembered Zion. On the willows there we hung up our harps. For there our captors asked us for songs of mirth, saying, 'Sing us one of the songs of Zion!'" (Ps 137:1–3).

But here's the rub. "How could we sing the Lord's song in a foreign land? If I forget you, O Jerusalem, let my tongue cling to the roof of my mouth, if I do not remember you, if I do not set Jerusalem above my highest joy" (vv. 4–6).

As to the mood and sentiment of the psalmist, one Hebraic scholar put it frankly:

> Since for the exiles there are no songs of Zion but the Lord's songs, the cruel request wounds their feelings, stirring afresh grief, homesickness, and indignation. To sing the Lord's songs in a strange land would be to desecrate them, for foreign lands were profane, "unclean" (cf. Amos 7:17; Hos 9:3–5). The thought of anyone singing the sacred songs to tickle the ears of a godless people evokes from the psalmist a passionate expression of his love for Jerusalem in the form of a curse on himself should he ever fail in loyalty to her. Sardonically, he offers a song with a string of curses (vv. 5–9) as a grim substitute for the request of the foe. He lays a curse on hand and tongue should they with lyre or song prove traitor to Jerusalem, which is higher than my highest joy.[19]

Oh, indeed, it would be nice if those Babylonian neighbors had overheard a Hebrew family or two worshipping Yahweh, and, being moved by the joyful noise and hopeful sound of their song, asked them to host a neighborhood hymn sing—and not in mockery but for real. Because undoubtedly the Babylonians were also hard-

---

[19]   William R. Taylor and W. Stewart McCullough, *The Interpreter's Bible* (New York: Abingdon Press, 1955), Vol. IV, "The Book of Psalms," 705–06.

pressed for joy, even if for reasons unlike those of the displaced Jerusalemites.

But the focus here is on the exiles, on the dispossessed within Babylon. And their response to the situation is but one breath short of blistering rage. Never, ever! Not outside of Jerusalem! Not beyond our holy city and the great temple! After all, the acoustics aren't so great down here by the river. And you Babylonians wouldn't understand the lyrics of our songs even if we sang them. Our language is not your language. They are our songs and we would prefer that our mouths be sealed shut forever rather than sing them for your sorry ears!

And then comes the blistering rage: "O daughter Babylon, you devastator! Happy shall they be who pay you back what you have done to us! Happy shall they be who take your little ones and dash them against the rock!" (vv. 8–9). End of psalm!

Life in exile can turn mighty nasty. It's a hard pill to swallow. But God had sent his beloved into Babylon to discipline them for rejecting to care for the poor, the fatherless, the widow, the stranger, and the alien. And now here they are, aliens themselves! In effect, God is saying to them: Since you haven't taken seriously my commandment to offer loving kindness to the strangers in your midst, I will place you in the midst of strangers for any kindness that they may offer you. And for seventy years it will be so! And, oh, by the way, you are to pray for them, your enemies. (Does that sound familiar to us Christians?) And that could have been the end of Jeremiah's prophecy. But it was only the half of it. And, the other half? God said to the exiles:

> When you call upon me and come and pray to me, I will hear you. When you search for me, you will find me; if you seek me with all your heart, I will let you find me . . . and I will restore your fortunes and gather you from all the nations and all the places where I have driven you . . . and I will bring you back to the place from which I sent you into exile. (Jer 29:12–14)

Presumably, then, seventy years would be ample time for the whole of Jeremiah's prophecy to sink in.

My grandfather Erie Renno always asked us to sing "Jesus Loves Me" at most of our family gatherings. It's such a simple, uncomplicated song. And Pap lived a life that made it clear he was singing this song not only at the church but to just about anyone who would listen. He took that song to places and people that other preachers such as he would not have gone. He sang this song for himself, his family, and for the world that God so loved and so loves still.

In a sermon I preached in 2007, I said, "Our Jerusalem (translate, church) is changing . . . Much of what we thought to be so important is disappearing . . . and some of us are fighting that . . . But if Babylon is going to prosper, then much of what we thought to be so sacred to us as God's people is going to have to change." And I noted that if we do not change, then "we too will experience a disintegration of all that we felt sacred about being the people of God . . . and we will be forced to rediscover what it means to be a blessing to the world, and once again recognize that this was God's plan all along as far back as Abraham and Sarah. Like them, we are called to be a sign and foretaste of the kingdom of God for the sake of Babylon . . . faithfully singing the shalom of God's peace in the places where God has carried us . . . as congregations, as individuals, and as families."

The question then is how we're going to sing the Lord's song in a foreign land when that land happens to be our own, in as much as its many different social, ethnic, cultural, and economic realities make strangers and aliens of us all. Can we "pray to the Lord on its behalf" and seek the welfare of others as our welfare? Can we pray and mean what we pray when we pray, "Your kingdom come. Your will be done, on earth as it is in heaven" (Matt 6:10)?

When we emerge from this current health and economic crisis into the new world that is coming, will our neighborhoods and our neighbors be better off because we finally began to pray for them and to sing God's songs with them? For that's radically different from wanting to dash the heads of their little ones against the rock. We might even agree to host hymn sings in our back yards. Maybe even our front yards. Which would give us a break from Facebook and all the rantings about who is to blame for the big mess we're in.

And speaking of the big mess we're in, and the fact that many of us have already hung up our harps on the willows and are left weeping for Jerusalem, how are we to accomplish the singing of the Lord's song?

It's really quite simple, if sometimes tearful. "When you call upon me and come and pray to me, I will hear you" (Jer 29:12).

CHAPTER EIGHTEEN

Saint Mark, Larry the Cable Guy, and Pink Floyd Hymns at a Mennonite Funeral

July 2020

Listening this evening to the hit song "There Will Be Days Like This" by Van Morrison, I was reminded of my dear friend Mark who had first introduced me to Van Morrison and given me a CD of the musician's hits. Mark recognized that Van Morrison was probably more in line with my musical preferences than his own favorite, Pink Floyd.

In any event, Mark was my neighbor and I was pretty sure he needed to talk to Jesus. What with that poster of a gun in his basement window, warning all who could see it that he believed in lethal force and just might use it, I figured that Jesus might be of some help to him. Fortunately or unfortunately, I could see the poster quite well from more than one angle of our property.

Mark was rarely to be seen. He slept during the day and stayed up wide awake at night. We had gotten to know his wife Peggy whom we met while walking the neighborhood when Heidi was recovering from ovarian cancer. Peggy jumped at the invitation to attend our congregation and soon became a member and one of the saints at Elizabethtown Mennonite.

But I was pretty sure that Mark was not up for sainthood, due to his rather colorful language, his black leather boots, and his generally unkempt look. He sported a considerably intimidating presence, and, of course, there was the menace of that poster sign of a gun pointing at my house.

Yet Mark, bless him, was one of the neighbors I had started praying for when we left the ministry in 2005. And I figured it was about time I should make an effort to meet the guy I was talking to Jesus about.

So, one day, seeing Mark in his back yard, I summoned the courage to yell, "Hi, Mark!" And that was all it took. From then on, a relationship formed between Mark and me. And I became responsible for telling Mark about Jesus. Why? Because, as I said, I was pretty sure Mark was in big need of Jesus.

Because Mark rarely came outdoors, and went about his business during his waking hours at night, he seemed to forget that the rest of us were not in conformity with his schedule. So he took it upon himself to begin calling me late at night, long after I was accustomed to having a coherent conversation. Nevertheless, if Jesus insisted that Mark be my personal project, then I could at least spend a few minutes with him from time to time despite the hour. I soon found our conversations to be uncommonly colorful and entertaining, and before I knew it, I became pretty fond of Mark.

One time (how could I forget?) he introduced me to Larry the Cable Guy with Larry's signature catchphrase, "Git-R-Done." Then he proceeded to tell me about some wildlife shows he'd been watching. And eventually, at a pivotal point, we approached matters of religion and questions of faith. Mark shared with me that he believed a variety of different things, but I didn't recall hearing Jesus in the list. This only confirmed for me once again that Mark needed to talk to Jesus.

Just as I needed to talk to Jesus, so did Mark! And frankly, believe it or not, we all do. So eventually I worked up my courage enough to ask Mark if I might pray for him. But, no, Mark was not interested. So, in a later late-night conversation, I tried again. And that time the answer was yes. So I prayed. And just as I was about to say "Amen," that deep and kind of gruff voice I had come to love began to pray and pray and pray and pray. And Mark prayed for me.

I'll never forget that prayer, because by the time he was done praying, I was pretty sure Mark already knew Jesus, at least a bit. And thus began the Mark and Conrad prayer meetings, in which it became increasingly clear, regardless of what Mark said, that he was somewhere along in his own journey with Jesus.

In the Spring of 2011, Heidi and I were candidating to return once again to the Elizabethtown Mennonite Church, after having resigned in 2005 from what turned out to be part one of our ministry there. We were torn about what to do when considering part two. But the night before we were to appear before the congregation to share our vision and answer questions, the phone rang about one hour past midnight, waking me from a deep sleep.

I knew who it was, and said, "Not tonight, Mark," and went back to sleep. Then phone call number two followed, and again I said, "Not tonight, Mark." And then finally, upon phone call number three, when it was clear that Mark was not going to stop calling until he got me up, I went downstairs and said, "Hello, Mark." To which Mark replied: "Conrad, I'm praying for you and I want you to know you are just the man for this job of pastor. I think you will do a great job."

That was about all I remembered, except for the fact that as I got off the phone, I thought to myself, there ain't nobody else up tonight praying for me, I'll bet, other than Saint Mark, my friend, the one I was so sure needed Jesus. Yet, I suspect that Jesus knew all along and chuckled about the fact that it was Mark who needed to be praying to Jesus for me, given that I was the one deliberating about coming back to Elizabethtown to preach on behalf of Jesus.

At times, between that telephone call in March 2011 and Mark's death on the first of July of that year, I would unexpectedly get a call from Mark, not at night but during the day. "Conrad I'm doing some cooking on my grill. I've got some hotdogs and I'm coming your way." And, sure enough, Mark showed up, and we shared the dogs and shot the breeze until Mark went home. Mark soon became seriously ill and was transferred to the hospital where I had my last visit with him and prayed for him. By then I was pretty sure Mark had become well acquainted with Jesus, and that Mark indeed had been on a journey with Jesus, and Jesus with Mark.

Had I helped to awaken what was—*Who* was—already resident within Mark? What exactly had been my role? I don't know that I'll ever know or need to know. But I do know that, for what little any of us actually know about most other people, we have no earthly idea as to who at any given moment "needs Jesus" and who doesn't. And just when we think Jesus may have brought someone to our attention who is in need of him, that is, in need of immediate salvation, be it bread for an empty stomach, water for a thirsty soul, or removal of a dangerous weapon aimed to kill, it's easy to overlook the moment of truth in our own lives when Jesus has something to say to us, too.

We hosted Mark's funeral at our Mennonite church, and we played Pink Floyd as folks gathered for the service. One of the saints jokingly suggested we should sanctify the sound system afterward. But what I knew was that Jesus had summoned Mark to help with sanctifying and preparing me for the past nine years of ministry. And during all of those years I have needed Mark's prayers more than I had any idea I would.

So, thank you, Mark, for being my friend, for loving me with all of my baggage, which probably intimidated you as much as you intimidated me. Thank you for loving me just as I am, just as Jesus does. It's been nine years now, and I still miss you and our late-night prayer meetings on the telephone.

CHAPTER NINETEEN

A Stressed-Out Preacher, a Knock at the Door, "Get the Hell Out!" and a Suspicious Neighbor Who Became My Trusted Friend
July 2021

As we prepared to move to our new neighborhood, we were warned about Cliff and his family. They never came out of their house. They dressed in black. Cliff drove a loud truck. And we didn't know where they came from or what they did with their time. You get the picture. It's the typical sort of stuff that people notice about other people who are different. That is, different to the extent that we don't bother to look beneath the assumptions we make about them. But to size people up without taking the time to consider what's really going on with them is hazardous to human relationships.

Let's say that they are Black and we are White. So *they* must be dangerous. Or, *they* are brown-skinned and we are white-skinned, so *they* must be "illegals" or drug dealers. Or, *they* are unemployed and we are employed, so *they* must have committed transgressions to get themselves fired. Or, *they* are on food stamps and we pay premium prices for groceries, so *they* must be Medicaid moochers. Or, we enjoy the benefits of a system that repeatedly works in our favor, but *they* must be milking the system for all it's worth.

That's how it happens. That's how those "others" become stereotypes upon whom we hang an invisible sign that reads, "I'm glad

I'm not like that!" Having labeled them for what we project upon them to be, rather than for what they are, we can then get back to the business at hand while keeping an eye on them just in case someday we need to call the police. It is as if we are the Pharisee "standing by himself," who said of the tax collector "standing far off," "God, I thank you that I am not like other people: thieves, rogues, adulterers, or even like this tax collector" (Luke 18:11). Half-truths about ourselves are easily exaggerated into falsities about somebody else.

Jesus refused, however, to accept half-truths and lies about anyone. And that included people like Zacchaeus the tax collector, the Samaritan woman at Jacob's well, the leper who begged to be healed of leprosy, the woman caught in adultery, the Gerasene demoniac living among the tombs, and even the Pharisees themselves who were in the habit of devouring widows' houses while for the sake of appearance made long prayers (Mt 23:14).

So one day I came home from a stressful time at the church. Let's just call it conflict since that's what it was. For one of the saints was unhappy with me, and I just wanted to escape. But what I heard when I got home was what we had heard way too often. Cliff and his wife and family were having a tumultuous day. And without even trying, they were informing the rest of the neighborhood. From the sound of it the conversation was painful for all concerned. But, painful or not, I decided I didn't want to hear any more yelling, despite the fact that it wasn't directed at me.

So without thinking much, I stepped over the fence that divided our yards and walked toward their house, where I knew that Cliff and his family might see me. I knocked on the door. And what I heard the very next moment was about as promising an assignment as any preacher might ever receive.

"Get the hell out of here!"

Needless to say, I didn't hesitate. And if only I could have delivered the goods by sending Hell packing along with me, I would have done so!

One day a week or so later, I was outdoors working, and so was Cliff. He, by the way, always kept everything spotlessly neat around his house. That is, everything except for the expletives.

I called out to him, "Hey Cliff!"

He looked up. "Was that you who came by our house last week?"

Yes, I nodded.

"I'm sorry for what I said. We were having a hard day."

"That's okay," I replied, "I was just thinking maybe I could help sort things out for you. You know, as a pastor. . . ."

Cliff stopped dead in his tracks. "O my God, you are a pastor?"

"I am."

He looked pretty shaken and turned as white as a sheet.

"I'm so sorry," he said, as if telling a pastor to get the hell out was somehow worse than telling the same to a neighbor who wasn't a pastor.

What Cliff hadn't realized yet was that while most of the saints around here think better than to use the H-word in front of the preacher, some of them have equally colorful ways of expressing themselves.

As Cliff turned toward me, he admitted, "My wife and I've been really struggling. I started reading my Bible a few weeks ago. And I'd like to come to church."

Now it's true that some folks around the church might think that Cliff didn't look much like church material. Why, with that stained white t-shirt, the black trousers, and always that black top hat on his head with the little ponytail sticking out the back, he was not dressed in what some would call his Sunday best. But I don't think Cliff gave a second thought to what kind of clothes he would wear to church. For he had something more pressing on his mind. And it was certainly more pressing than what the saints at the church might have thought about him. For he was waiting to hear something besides presumptuous conclusions about what he ought to look like when he was always used to looking just like himself.

Cliff waited much like the Ethiopian eunuch who was seated in his chariot while reading the prophet Isaiah. The apostle Philip asked the eunuch, "Do you understand what you are reading?" The eunuch answered, "How can I, unless someone guides me?" (Acts 8:27–31). And strange though it may seem, I'm pretty sure that the Holy Spirit plopped me down into Cliff's life just like "the Spirit said to Philip, 'Go over to this chariot and join it'" (v. 29). And while there's no textual evidence to suggest that the eunuch used the H-word to scoot Philip away in the same manner that Cliff employed the word against me, the end result was the same. Both the eunuch and Cliff got introduced to Jesus.

Consequently, despite being newly discovered of Jesus some two thousand years apart from each other, the eunuch and Cliff very soon received the Lord's baptism. So I definitely believe it when the psalmist says, "For a thousand years in your sight are like yesterday when it is past" (Ps 90:4a). Our yesterdays are but a brief foreshadowing of someone else's tomorrow.

Cliff became an active member of our congregation. Every Sunday until he and his family moved out of town several years later, Cliff sat right beside Heidi and me in the second row at the front of the church. Needless to say, I miss Cliff. He fast became one of my best friends. He grew in his understanding of what it meant to follow Jesus. He reconciled with his family. He made peace where there had long been division. He regularly read from *Our Daily Bread*[20] and couldn't figure out for the life of him why we didn't distribute its

---

[20]   https://ourdailybread.org/read/.

gems to the good folk at church. So he ordered them for us and we still read them today.

Cliff was yet another saint that Jesus had brought my way. Much like the Greeks who said to Philip, "Sir, we wish to see Jesus" (John 12:21b), Cliff sought Jesus, just as I sought Cliff. And it was by that same Spirit who got me to talking to "Saint" Mark with the gun poster in his window. Who would have thought?

Our congregation was going through some painful conflict, and I was at the center of much of the tension. Many Sundays, I wasn't sure if I had any allies or not. But I knew when Cliff came down the aisle and sat beside me, and put his arm around me, that I had at least three allies that morning—Heidi, Cliff, and the Holy One who had brought Cliff and me together. No matter what anyone said about me, Cliff was evidence enough that I was still hearing from God, and evidence enough as well that God was still at work in my life and using me for his purposes. That fact alone, along with Heidi's prayer before the sermon, gave me courage to preach yet one more Sunday.

As I said, I greatly miss Cliff. He helped me see again that we only slight ourselves when we write people off because they are different—for being Black or Brown or Gay or poor or uneducated—or because they reside somewhere on the autism spectrum—or because they struggle with mental illness—or because they've committed some terrible crime—or because they don't look at all like church material, whatever that is supposed to be, other than what it is.

Saints such as Cliff and company don't wear their accomplishments on the outside. But wow, are they ever beautiful on the inside! You know, as well as I, that believing or repeating stereotypes about people never lets us know the deep-down truths in them. But Jesus knows them all. So we saints, every time we are about to make half-baked judgments about somebody, need to be like the Greeks who

said to Philip, "Sir, we wish to see Jesus," since Jesus has an even better chance than we do of changing our minds.

Glory, "Saint" Cliff! Glory in the fact that the next time you
see me, Saint Peter will be saying to you, "Go over there to Conrad's
chariot and join it!"

I'll surely need your company.

CHAPTER TWENTY

"Got" Jesus? Regardless of How You Answer, Your Life Is Sacred
July 2020

I've had the blessing of teaching at Elizabethtown College for nearly three decades, interacting year-after-year with the most delightful students a professor could imagine. One of my favorite courses is the one entitled Discovering Society, in which I introduce the basics of sociology.

From the very beginning of my teaching career, when I wasn't so far from the students' ages myself, my goal was to speak to the basics of what it means to be a human being. And why? Because if I couldn't convey at least that much, then anything else I conveyed would hardly matter.

From my observations of them, I would regularly tell them that the most successful among them possess three qualities in common. They work harder than others. They take risks no one else is willing to take. And they "walk the talk," by which I mean that they live with integrity and tell the truth. So I would say to them, "You can have the first two qualities of hard work and risk-taking and yet still end up in the police report or in the obituary section of the newspaper sooner than you need to. But if you have the third, and 'walk the talk,' then you're going to do just fine because the world is dying for people like this."

From the very outset I've also taught my students that their lives are sacred. From my theological perspective, this means they were created sacred and that therefore their flesh and bones are sacred, as are their daily and lifetime journeys. This I believe with all of my heart. Regardless of their religious commitments, or lack of them, or their sexual orientations, their experiences of trauma, their criminal records, their emotional and mental health challenges, or their race or ethnicity—each one of them is a sacred person.

To work with this most vital of beliefs, I initially ask students to read Frederick Buechner's earliest memoir, *The Sacred Journey*.[21] Buechner spent his life as a teacher, ordained minister, and prolific writer. He is certainly one of the most honest authors I've ever read, as is Anne Lamott.[22] Buechner's point is that God is always speaking to each of us, and that our lives bear the mark of God's sacredness within us.

What do I mean by sacred? In human terms, the sacred is that which is set apart as far more special than the everyday throw-away stuff of our lives. It's like the expensive dishes behind the glass window of the china closet, or the occasions upon which we dress up in all our finery for grieving our sorrows and celebrating our joys, or the breaking of the bread and lifting of the cup at the communion table to eat and drink of the One who came and lived and died to say just how much we are loved.

The problem for us Christians is that we truly forget that "God so loved the world" (John 3:16a), meaning that it literally is the world (the kosmos) that God loves. While we teach our children this familiar verse early in life, too often we turn right around and live as if the verse reads, "God so loved the special people of the church." Without saying so, we imply that the rest of the world can go you know where! Our insider's language spells a tale of those poor souls outside of the church who just haven't gotten their stuff together yet,

---

[21]   Frederick Buechner, *The Sacred Journey* (San Francisco: Harper & Row, Publishers, 1982). See https://www.frederickbuechner.com/.

[22]   https://barclayagency.com/speakers/anne-lamott/.

and we aren't sure they ever will. Yet we will pray for them after we finish shaking our heads and talking about them.

The underlying issue then for us is that we may act as if a person's life becomes sacred only after choosing to love God, when in actuality "we love because he first loved us" (I John 4:19). The psalmist sings of it.

> For it was you who formed my inner parts;
>   you knit me together in my mother's womb.
> I praise you, for I am fearfully and wonderfully made.
>   Wonderful are your works;
> that I know very well.
>   My frame was not hidden from you,
> when I was being made in secret,
>   intricately woven in the depths of the earth.
> Your eyes beheld my unformed substance.
> In your book were written
>   all the days that were formed for me,
>   when none of them as yet existed. (Ps 139:13–16)

Folks, this is more than poetic truth, for it is the ultimate truth that pertains to each and every person that God has created. Every single one of us is a sacred creature of God's own making, with the sweetness of God's breath breathing life into us. This is true whether we have chosen to live our lives for God's good sake or not, which presumably is what some people imply by asking, "Have you 'got' Jesus?"

I think that we who say we love Jesus would have infinitely more credibility if our love for Jesus revealed in us the ways by which Jesus universally loves. For then we would begin to see that same love appearing within our families, friends, neighbors, and coworkers, regardless of whether or not they've "got" Jesus. Some of them might even dare to ask us about the hope that is within us.

Living and interacting with thousands of students across these decades has only increased my love and care for them as the sacred treasures they are in God's sight. I make it my task to encourage them in what is true and good, to call out the gifts God has placed within them, to share whatever wisdom I can from my own hard knocks, failures, and suffering, and to pass on to them my belief that their very being is of far more value than they may yet realize, especially when encountering frustration, doubt, discouragement, or untimely death, tragedy, or illness. For there is a sacred hope within them, whether conscious or unconscious, just as there is in all of us.

Having been diagnosed with Parkinson's disease has only strengthened the bonds that I feel with my students. There is something about an old guy with a PhD, tremoring as he is in the classroom, that creates a connection with eighteen- and twenty-year-olds who may not tremor on the outside but are quick to acknowledge they tremor on the inside. And so it is that I'm not shy about sharing with them my faith and trust in the One in whom I place my own hope, in the assurance that I, too, like them, am of far greater worth than on those days when I feel that I am not.

What I know is this. Every semester I have a classroom full of students who bear the distinct mark of God upon them, set apart and given a name uniquely their own, and loved with a sacred love that is from the foundation of the world, offered to them at the very moment of their birth. This means that I am called to love them just as Jesus loves them. And who knows? Maybe one or two or more of them will someday surprise themselves by saying, "I think I've 'got' Jesus." Or, more accurately, Jesus will have "gotten" hold of them in the sense of the prayer that he himself prayed to God:

"I have made your name known to those whom you gave me from the world. They were yours, and you gave them to me, and they have kept your word" (John 17:6).

CHAPTER TWENTY-ONE

Why "You Can't Get to Heaven by Being Good" Is Not the Good News!

June 2020

Most of us who have grown up in Evangelical circles have heard something like this or even repeated it: "You don't get to heaven by being a good person" or "your goodness won't save you" or "what good you do doesn't matter for your salvation."

Usually we make these declarations when we are talking to a stranger, neighbor, or friend who is asking questions about the Christian faith, or who may feel some compulsion to please us by ratifying whatever we happen to say, whether it be the "gospel truth" or not. So let's think about this for a minute. What are we really saying at such times? How might we be heard and interpreted? Perhaps, something like the following:

Friend, you are a schmuck and a loser and have been a schmuck and a loser all of your life, and Jesus doesn't want schmucks and losers in his kingdom. Your only chance of becoming a non-schmuck or non-loser is for you to give your life to Jesus so you can become just like the rest of us who are saints.

Or, neighbor, nothing you've done in your life up to this point matters, regardless of how much good you've done and how faithful you've been in your relationships, or what good accomplishments you've achieved, or how generous you've been to the poor, or how often you've been a good neighbor. No, you are a "bad apple." And the only hope for you to be a "good apple"—a saint—is to profess faith in Jesus and become a Christian. *Got that?*

But there's definitely a problem here, isn't there? That is, a problem with this approach to being a Christian. For it implicitly assumes that we human beings are innately defective to begin with, which is to say, imprisoned in a state of total corruption from the day of our creation, regardless of our good thoughts and good deeds. Accordingly, we are condemned to this state of depravity unless we are "saved" by consciously professing faith in Jesus.

Scripture, however, has a different take on human nature. The opening creation narrative of the book of Genesis repeatedly asserts that "God saw everything that he had made, and indeed, it was very good" (Gen 1:31a; see vv. 1–31). That includes especially us humans.

To be sure, succeeding passages in Genesis and other books of the Old and New Testaments depict the reality of human sin. Adam's and Eve's explicit disobedience of God adds considerable complication to the picture of human life within and beyond the Garden of Eden. Yet, sin and evil do not invalidate or nullify what God has called good. Rather, they obscure it. We still remain wonderfully made in God's own image (Gen 5:1b; 9:6b).

That's why a "bad apple" conception of human nature, which typifies some versions of Evangelical Christianity, is not born of the gospel. For the starting point, end point, and center point of biblical faith is not bad news. It is good news. The New Testament word *euaggelion*, from which comes the English "evangelical," and which also translates as "gospel" (good spiel), means a message of good news. The gospel of Jesus Christ is then the celebrative news that corresponds to God's bestowal of "good" upon all creatures at the very moment of creation. It is the manifestation of God's all-encompassing "blessing" throughout the created order and in all of human history (Gen 1:28a).

The opening sentences of the Gospel of John, which parallel the opening words of Genesis, confirm this good news.

> In the beginning was the Word, and the Word was with God, and the Word was God. He was in the beginning with God. All things came into being through him, and without him not one thing came into being. What has come into being in him was life, and the life was the light of all people. The light shines in the darkness, and the darkness did not overcome it."
> (John 1:1–5)

"The darkness did not overcome it" is John's declaration that the light of God's goodness as seen in Jesus Christ is forever and always present to us even when that goodness is momentarily obscured. Consequently:

The chief tax collector Zacchaeus, whose corrupt ways obscure the goodness in which he was created, is transformed by the good news of the light of Christ, turning Zacchaeus from a life of thievery to a fourfold restitution of what is good for those whom he has defrauded (Luke 19:1–10).

The leper who begs to be cleansed of his leprosy receives overwhelmingly good news as Jesus touches and heals him, restoring him to the community that has shunned, banished, and dismissed him as untouchable (Mark 1:40–45, Matt 8:1–4, Luke 5:12–16).

The woman caught in adultery by the scribes and Pharisees rejoices in the extraordinarily good news that, when all is about to be lost, she is suddenly liberated from the condemnation of her male accusers. Their own darkness in sin, when exposed to the light of Christ, grants them no ground upon which to cast the first stone. Just so, Jesus declares to her, "Neither do I condemn you," and frees her from the life of adultery that could not have been hers to begin with apart from the sins of men, who in this instance are also freed from their darkest desire to kill her (John 8:1–11).

The Gerasene demoniac, whose name is Legion, is loosened from the shackles and chains that bind him naked among the tombs, which is unbelievable to him as good news until the unclean spirit within him comes out at Jesus's command. Then it is believable. For the first time in his life he celebrates the goodness of life for which he was created, proclaiming his gratitude by saying "how much Jesus had done for him; and everyone was amazed" (Luke 8:26–29, Mark 5:1–20, Matt 8:28–34).

Good news gospel! And the list of amazements goes on! For with Jesus there is no "bad-apple" theology. The goodness of God's infinite love is forever and always at work in and through the risen, cosmic Christ. So, we Evangelicals should not be surprised when those who are not consciously or explicitly followers of Jesus display kindness, generosity, care, empathy, compassion, and sacrificial love. For these good gifts come to them from the same Spirit of the same God who bestows such graces upon everyone at the creation, graces that show up everywhere, including in you and me at our darkest hour. "God is love, and those who abide in love abide in God, and God abides in them" (1 John 4:16b). "In this is love, not that we loved God but that he loved us and sent his Son to be the atoning sacrifice for our sins" (v. 10).

With that being said, there is no need for false assumptions about our human goodness, as though on the one hand it can be of no consequence, and that on the other hand we Christians are the only ones who possess it. From the day we are born to the day we die, the goodness we receive from God is always a gift of grace. Grace is not exclusive to us, nor is it excluding of others. Christ's community is not a country club for the "saved" elite. It is a deep well from which any and all may drink of the "living water" of love's goodness as a universal birthright. It comes straight to us from God at the beginning, in the present, and at the end of our existence, as confirmed by the life, death, and resurrection of Jesus Christ. It is non-Christians who sometimes help us Christians to see this. And that's for the simple reason that God's goodness can just as easily appear in them as be obscured in us. Besides, who are we to say that our own goodness is to no avail, or that our unrighteousness cannot be turned to good ends?

"He makes his sun rise on the evil and on the good, and sends rain on the righteous and on the unrighteous" (Matt 5:45). And this is very good news, including for those of us to whom it may seem offensive. So, what might happen if we who have received the gift of God's grace were to view all of those around us, not as "bad apples" to be saved from falling into the pit of hell, but as beloved children of God whom we invite to be our sisters, brothers, neighbors, and friends on the journey to God's new Jerusalem? For then we would recognize and affirm the gifts of God's goodness that are already present in them, even if for the time being they are temporarily obscured.

CHAPTER TWENTY-TWO

"I Feel Like Such a Schmuck," Yet Jesus Loved Schmucks and Became One of Them

August 2020

A listener to one of my podcasts responded to me on Facebook by saying that the personal challenges he has faced in life seemed like small potatoes in comparison with mine, which made him feel like a schmuck.

A schmuck is a person who for some reason feels foolish to himself, or even for reasons beyond his control may appear foolish to others. So in reply to my listener, I said something to the tune of, "The good news is that we are all schmucks in some way, and that Jesus has a preference for schmucks. In fact, he has a knack for finding and hanging out with them in every town he visits."

So, does this mean then that Jesus has a desire to hang out with you and me? When I'm in doubt, it helps me to think about it while reading and praying. From what we find in the four New Testament Gospels, would you agree with me that Jesus felt especially comfortable in the company of the world's afflicted? And, was he not also quite comfortable in the company of those who, believing themselves to be unafflicted, felt uncomfortable when in the company of the so-obviously afflicted? It's true that Jesus had a profound affinity for any and all who by habit were used to ducking their heads in the midst of a crowd. And also for those who instinctively ran away from the scene whenever they couldn't stand being surrounded by the super-comfortable, super-righteous, and super-religious types who showed subtle but not-so-subtle contempt for them.

We've already named a few of those who must have felt like schmucks—given their reputations for being the "bad apples" around town. Folks like Zacchaeus the chief tax collector, despised in his community, and the unclean leper ostracized from his community, and the adulterous woman shamed by her community, and the Gerasene demoniac, whose numbers are "Legion," warded off, locked up, and left for dead in communities the world over.

Can we imagine? Can we imagine just how the physically, socially, and economically afflicted so often feel? How they bluster, bluff, and sputter their way around, and pick and roll for one another, and at the end of the day are met by the glaring glances of highly advantaged people who shun and pity them as schmucks of the world? Constant contempt, constant ostracism, constant shame, and flat-out abandonment can eventually do a person in. And so can looking with condescension and disdain upon someone else's affliction. For sooner or later it can make schmucks of us all, including you and me. It depends upon whether we see our own faces in their faces, upon whether we can no longer hide our own vulnerability behind the veneer of righteousness, riches, and privileges, since none of these things can finally protect any us from being schmucked ourselves.

The prophet Isaiah painted a vivid picture of what a real schmuck looks like.

> He had no form or majesty that we should look at him, nothing in his appearance that we should desire him. He was despised and rejected by others; a man of suffering and acquainted with infirmity; and as one from whom others hide their faces he was despised, and we held him of no account. (Isa 53:2b–3)

That, too, was the likeness of Jesus.

Saint Paul once defined his own likeness—his former self named Saul—as the chief of sinners (I Tim 1:15, KJV). A sorry schmuck of a Pharisee, he had swindled people of their very flesh-and-blood by "breathing threats and murder against the disciples of the Lord." With letters for their extradition in hand, Saul had headed up to the synagogues of Damascus to bring "any who belonged to the Way, men or women" back to Jerusalem, to be hauled before the executioner and put to death (Acts 9:1ff).

With the divine goodness obscured within Saul, his heart and mind remained darkened. But then, "suddenly a light from heaven flashed around him" and struck him down. His Pharisaical virtues came to naught. He stood blind before Christ. He could not yet "see" when Jesus asked him, "Saul, Saul, why do you persecute me?" It's an eye-popping question that could cause any one of us to go blind.

"Why do you persecute me?" by creating tax havens for the rich while depriving the poor of a decent day's wage? "Why do you persecute me?" by dropping bombs on homes and hospitals instead of offering bread to hungry stomachs and water to thirsty mouths? "Why do you persecute me?" by locking up children in wire cages instead of caressing them in the comfort of sheltering arms and hands? "Why do you persecute me?" by praising dictators instead of summoning release of the oppressed from the grip of the oppressor?

It is true that Jesus is always concerned for those who are treated as the schmucks of the world. In his letters to the seven churches in the book of Revelation, the beloved disciple John conveyed admonitions from the risen Christ to those angel-messengers of congregations in Ephesus, Smyrna, Pergamum, Thyatira, Sardis, Philadelphia, and Laodicea. Each of the letters began with the same words: "I know your works."

In the case of the seventh letter to the church at Laodicea, the risen Lord said:

> "I Know your works; you are neither cold nor hot. I wish that you were either cold or hot. So, because you are lukewarm, and neither cold nor hot, I am about to spit you out of my mouth. For you say, 'I am rich, I have prospered, and I need nothing.' You do not realize that you are wretched, pitiable, poor, blind, and naked. Therefore I counsel you to buy from me gold refined by fire so that you may be rich; and white robes to clothe you and to keep the shame of your nakedness from being seen; and salve to anoint your eyes so that you may see. I reprove and discipline those whom I love. Be earnest, therefore, and repent." (Rev 3:15–19)

As a kid, I used to live in tremendous fear that I was a member of the church of Laodicea. I think revival preachers loved touting that passage from Revelation. But what most of them forgot to share with us, because they were so heavy on the condemnation that comes with being lukewarm, was that Laodicea is the only church of the seven to which Jesus said, following his admonition to repent, "I am standing at the door, knocking; if you hear my voice and open the door, I will come in to you and eat with you, and you with me" (3:20).

Which is to say, if we open the door, he will remove the curse of schmuckdom and provide us instead with all the necessary provisions of his kingdom—his true riches, clothing that forever removes the shame of our nakedness, and sight that once and for all sheds our willful blindness, along with every other thing that afflicts us.

Just as Jesus did for the detested Zacchaeus, for the unclean leper, for the adulterous woman shamed by her accusers, for the crazed Gerasene demoniac among the tombs, and for Saul, that "bad apple" Pharisee whom the risen Christ re-sanctified as Saint Paul, who then declared: "For that very reason I have received mercy, so that in me as the foremost [of sinners], Jesus Christ might display the utmost patience, making me an example to those who would come to believe in him for eternal life" (I Tim 1:16).

What more could anyone possibly want and receive? By no means are such mercies small potatoes.

CHAPTER TWENTY-THREE

A Church Built on Lies and a Person Who Believed Those Lies Until He Didn't
August 2020

As I said, when I was a kid, I was captivated by images from Isaiah 40, describing an excavation project for which the voice of the prophet calls out: "In the wilderness prepare the way of the Lord, make straight in the desert a highway for our God. Every valley shall be lifted up, and every mountain and hill be made low; the uneven ground shall become level, and the rough places a plain." For "then the glory of the Lord shall be revealed, and all people shall see it together" (Isa 40:3–5b).

What an exhilarating scene to behold! The allusion is to the procession of an ancient king who makes his way through the desert in order to reach and redeem his people from their captivity in exile—except in this case it is not just any king. For it is the Lord God Yahweh himself, whose *kabod*, whose glory, will be manifest before all the people.

All barriers to his entry must be removed: mountains and hills laid low, valleys lifted up, rough ground smoothed out, and rugged terrain opened up. Isaiah's overarching theme is that whatever prevents God's presence from being felt and God's purposes from being fulfilled must be dismantled. And whatever provides support for God's actions must be built up. For God has come to set right the things that have gone wrong, which includes every lie that seeks to falsify the truth of God's ways in the world. For it is God's kingdom that will prevail among the kingdoms of the earth.

As I look back on what I've written over the past year, I realize how often I have revisited many of the lies I had come to believe about myself, about God, and about the world that God so greatly loves. And also how much I sought to exorcise those lies so that "the glory of God in the face of Jesus Christ" (2 Cor 4:6) might be more fully revealed through my life and yours.

Noah benShea tells the story of how we proceed through our lives. Slowly we build walls of stones, stones that are the lies we've come to believe, lies we've been told, and lies we've repeated. But as we grow old, we begin to recognize how such walls have prevented us from seeing the truth of the world around us, so that the work of growing old is the work of tearing down those walls.[23]

Looking back, this summer has been for me that kind of work, or at least its beginning, with yet a long way to go. I am honored that so many of you have tuned in to hear me reflect, and I trust that some of the things I've shared have been of use to you in your own excavation project, a project that Saint Paul describes as the working out of our salvation with fear and trembling (Phil 2:12).

Brené Brown, in a recent book entitled *Dare to Lead*, writes about the stories we tell—stories about others, stories about God, and invariably stories about ourselves that often are only partly true and sometimes completely false.[24]

Just so, we have inherited a church that over the centuries has fabricated its own lies, and we have added more lies to those lies. We have gone so far as to create a theology of lies. We have preached those lies. We have told our children those lies. Most devastatingly, we have actually believed those lies. And I, too, have preached those lies, much to my regret.

What, then, are the worst lies upon which a misguided church

---

23   Noah benShea, *Jacob the Baker* (New York: Ballantine Books, 1990).
24   Brené Brown, *Dare to Lead* (New York: Random House, 2018).

has been built, and by which our lives have been wrongly shaped and molded? They are those mountains and hills of deception that are to be brought low, those uneven places to be straightened out as the Holy Spirit dismantles a mis-directed church, and those falsifications of truth that we, being called to be faithful, are to renounce and toss into the bottomless pit from which they came.

Foremost is the lie that Jesus came to save us from the everlasting wrath of God. I heard that lie repeated just this morning in a contemporary, supposedly Christian song about Psalm 90, by Shane and Shane[25]—saying that God has directed his wrath toward his children, but, lucky for us, Jesus stepped into the picture to rescue us from that wrath. What rubbish!

First of all, Jesus is the Son of God, the Word of God, who "was in the beginning with God" (John 1:2). "All things came into being through him, and without him not one thing came into being," as the opening of John's Gospel declares (v. 3). This very same Gospel also affirms that "God so loved the world that he gave his only Son, so that everyone who believes in him may not perish but have eternal life" (v. 3:16).

The New Testament churches from their beginning rightly asserted that this one God-in-three-persons—Father, Son, and Holy Spirit—is not trifurcated into disparate parts of God turned against one another. Rather each and all aspects of the one God live and work—from, within, and toward one another. God is not at war with God, for the heart of God is love and God is unified in love.

Moreover, God's wrath cannot be separated from God's love as though God's wrath requires appeasement, requital, and sacrificial satisfaction, as people are wont to claim when they sever God's wrath from God's love. The apostle John states succinctly, "God is love, and those who abide in love abide in God, and God abides in them"

---

25   https://www.azlyrics.com/lyrics/shaneshane/psalm90.html/.

(1 John 4:16). "There is no fear in love, but perfect love casts out fear; for fear has to do with punishment, and whoever fears has not reached perfection in love" (v. 18). Wrath, not love, begets fear. The apostle Paul asserts in his earliest letter, "God has destined us not for wrath but for obtaining salvation through our Lord Jesus Christ" (1 Thess 5:9).

A central lie perpetuated by the church is the belief that God is forever angry with us. This lie was at the core of hell-fire and brimstone messages I heard as a kid during revival meetings, to which I responded by trudging up the aisle for one invitation after another, not knowing what in the world I had done. Again and again, I needed to shame myself in front of five hundred people, as though I was hedging my bets at every chance I could get, in case George Brunk II was right, that God was constantly pissed at me. I couldn't count on what I heard about God, except for the further bludgeoning of me with the lie that so many of us carry deep down inside, which is the internalized wrath that says, I am no good, no earthly good at all.

Tragically, as a consequence, this is the same message that far too many people pass on to their children, so that their children then come to believe that they also are of no earthly good either.

So, let me ask you. Does that self-decrying, self-condemning, self-loathing message of wrath sound like it comes from the mouth of Jesus? This is what Jesus said in his own prayer to God:

> "As you, Father, are in me and I am in you, may they also be in us . . . I in them and you in me, that they may become completely one, so that the world may know that you have sent me and have loved them even as you have loved me. Father, I desire that those also, whom you have given me, may be with me where I am, to see my glory, which you have given me because you loved me before the foundation of the world." (John 17:21–24)

Does this prayer bear witness to God's endless wrath, or to God's everlasting love? Sadly, believing that God was chiefly angry with me led me to see the Lord's table as a source of reproach and sure damnation, rather than of certain salvation—as a place I could approach only if I first attained sufficient perfection to demolish all of my imperfection, no matter how great or small. The communion table was not a joyful place for me to receive Christ's body broken for me and Christ's blood shed for me, but instead a fearsome place where, for the life of me, I could not see myself as Christ had prayed for me: *Christ in me, and I in Christ.*

Folks, irrespective of what I formerly believed about the endless wrath of God, we gather at the Lord's table in a re-presentation of the drama of God's unconditional love. The eucharist is a re-enactment of our salvation as the greatest story ever told. It is the promise of that moment when the thief who hung on the cross next to Jesus turned to him and said, "Jesus, remember me when you come into your kingdom." And Jesus replied, "Truly I tell you, today you will be with me in Paradise" (Luke 23:42–43).

For just as in the wilderness a highway was prepared for the coming of the Lord, so too here at the table of grace the King of heaven prepares his feast for us, so that all of God's people may experience the splendor of his love revealed in all of his glory.

PART FIVE

MINISTRY IN A CHURCH DISMANTLED

CHAPTER TWENTY-FOUR

The Trouble with Pastors Who Are Troubled and Who Trouble
May 2020

Back in 2007 or 2008, when I was in the midst of speaking about my book *Road Signs for the Journey*, someone asked me, "What is the biggest challenge facing the church?" Without hesitation I noted "the professionalization of the clergy."

In making this claim I was not blaming pastors for a system they were not entirely responsible for creating. Rather, I was critiquing the "church-industrial complex" that defined and constructed a work-world in which we thought the only way to be an effective pastor is to spend seven years in higher education and about $100,000 to do so, plus official credentialing equivalent to that of other professionals.

What I meant back then was that we have created a model of ministry for the church that in many respects mirrors the dynamics of the market-driven "military-industrial complex" which balances its budgets on a permanent commitment to war that keeps the defense manufacturing factories humming.

By way of further analogy to such social complexes, the professionalized clergy model bears resemblance to the "prison-industrial complex" that re-classifies old behaviors as new "crimes" in order to create steeper penalties for keeping prisons filled with prisoners serving longer sentences. The hires of private corporations are "credentialed" (however minimally) to work the prison system, not unlike highly educated and intensively trained physicians and nurses who are credentialed to serve the for-profit and not-for-profit healthcare systems.

The broader social fabric is composed of a network of interconnected industrial complexes, making it increasingly improbable if not impossible for the leadership of ecclesiastical institutions to differentiate themselves from this giant spider's web. The result is a conglomeration of voluntary, consumer-driven, cafeteria-modelled, and loosely affiliated competing religions of diverse persuasions, including the market-mimicking, "prosperity gospel" churches. As with every other institution that forages for a slice of the population pie, universal forces and factions determine whether churches live or die. The proverbial butterfly that flaps its wings in California causes a breeze to stir the gnats in Pennsylvania.

My point is not to say that there are exact equivalencies between the dynamics of religious and secular fiefdoms within the larger megacomplex, but rather that a common pecuniary thread runs through them. Namely, whenever an enterprise feeds upon itself until it no longer has the financial or human wherewithal to sustain its appetite, it is subject inevitably to the law of diminishing returns. All consumer-driven and market-driven economies, whether branded as religious or secular, suffer when they lose their customer bases, just as political idols fall out of favor when they lose their adherents.

Within academic fields the same cyclical currents of growth and attrition are at work. Academia is part and parcel of the larger "university-governmental-industrial complex." A person with a four-year baccalaureate degree, plus a master's degree, plus a PhD, say, in English literature, American history, or the science of earthworm genetics, has no guarantee of obtaining or retaining stable employment, though the odds significantly favor the earthworm scientist. Yet whoever may happen to cross the threshold into the classroom or research lab, with all of the requisite professional designations and certifications in hand, is virtually assured of accumulating a gargantuan personal debt-to-income ratio for years to come. Meanwhile, institutions of higher learning, many of which depend upon governmental, military, and industrial allocations, watch their proceeds from tuition fees and endowments suffer a rapidly diminishing half-life.

Plopped down in the middle of all of these complexes are churches and their pastors—the holy lot of them. They must subsist on the voluntarism of charitable giving, which as the heartbeat of all benevolent enterprises represents a shrinking slice of the economic pie (leaving aside those televangelists who prey upon the pocketbooks of the theologically naive and emotionally vulnerable).

So when we talk about debt-laden preachers and pastors as "professionals," whose salaries do not rise nearly so high as their steepled edifices, we are describing a class of dedicated servants who oversee congregational and missional budgets that in many instances are dwindling down to the hour when the sign above the padlocked door reads, "Closed." Moreover, the time for shuttering the windows may accelerate rapidly whenever prophetic words, like the "jeremiads" of Jeremiah, come from the mouths of preachers who preach the hard truths and teachings, as well as the immeasurable blessings, of the gospel of Jesus Christ. As Jesus himself said, "Woe to you when all speak well of you, for that is what their ancestors did to the false prophets" (Luke 6:26).

So, a conversation between a pastor and congregation at the conclusion of a post-Covid Sabbath worship service might commence something like this:

"Preacher, we don't like what we've heard you say today! Why do you trouble us? Like Jeremiah who railed against the cultic idols of his day, you take aim at the corporate capitalists who deposit our paychecks in the bank. Do you really think we're as bad as those people of Jerusalem who placed their children as burnt offerings upon the altars of Baal (Jer 19:4–5, 9:12–14)? Surely, you're not saying anything like that, are you?"

"No, I'm not saying that! But what I am asking all of us to think seriously about is this: Upon what altars do we in fact sacrifice our children and our children's children within the megacomplex of *today's* cultural idols?"

In Jeremiah's day, Judah was entangled in a socio-economic-political-ecclesiastical-complex of foreign and domestic alliances it believed would guarantee its national safety and sovereignty, which included sacrifices offered to foreign gods. All the while, its "professional" guild of prophets (clergy) were preaching peace when there was no peace. Meanwhile, God's people collectively neglected the alien, the orphan, and the widow in their midst (Jer 7:5–7). So Jeremiah announced that Yahweh-God would dismantle Judah's institutions and customary ways of living as a consequence of their forsaking the commandments of God.

> My people have forgotten me, they burn offerings to a delusion; they have stumbled in their ways, in the ancient roads, and have gone into bypaths, not the highway, making their land a horror, a thing to be hissed at forever. All who pass by it are horrified and shake their heads. Like the wind from the east, I will scatter them before the enemy. I will show them my back, not my face, in the day of their calamity. (Jer 18:15–17)

When, out of faithfulness to God, Jeremiah mocked the priestly "professionals" of Judah for their perfidy, Jeremiah's accusers threw him in jail. Yet, the priestly "professionals" stood in far greater jeopardy with God, for they had led the politicians and people astray by falsely blessing Judah's abandonment of Yahweh.

Today, in a similar vein, the church and those of us who are its leaders forsake the commandments of God whenever we pledge allegiance in support of systems of oppression, militarism, racism, greed, gun-mania, and wars of violence. It's upon these altars that a nation sacrifices its children while in wholesale fashion neglecting the alien, the orphan, the widow, and the poor. It is the faithful pastor and congregation—faithful to God—who are caught in the crosscurrents.

Like Jeremiah, we pastors are a troubled lot, and we are especially troubled as the social fabric unravels at the seams. For this land, too, like Judah in Jeremiah's time, is filled with many idols that lure God's people away from doing the will of God. Perhaps, then, we pastors must begin by admitting, with Jeremiah: "Ah, Lord God! Truly I do not know how to speak, for I am only a fledgling" (Jer 1:6).[26]

So then, we call the saints to gather in Jesus's presence, and together we ask him: Where are you, Lord, with all of this? What would you have us do? How are we to follow in your footsteps?

Then we pray and wait for the Spirit to show us.

---

[26]   "Fledgling" is a paraphrastic noun for the Hebrew *na'ar*, boy.

CHAPTER TWENTY-FIVE

Pandemic Pastors: Will We Make It to the Tipping Point or Fall Flat First?
July 2020

For the last day or so I have found my thought shifting from the phrase "the dismantling of the church" to "the dismantled church." That may be only a subtle semantic shift, yet it occurred to me after having breakfast with a good friend who noted that Andy Stanley had just announced that his Atlanta congregation would not assemble for worship throughout the rest of the year.

During a recent meeting of our own congregation, I had a related thought about when we might assemble again. Obviously, I didn't know. But I did wonder as to what the Spirit's metric would look like with respect to God's dismantling. I know that my own metric suggests we are already pretty close to being dismantled, with each passing day bringing greater uncertainty regarding just about everything. How far might the Spirit take this whole process of coming apart at the seams?

I have to confess that for all of my big talk over the past two months, about waiting to reassemble only after we've done the hard work of discerning the will of the Spirit, I found myself missing the saints and feeling unsure as to what it means to be a pandemic pastor. How does one minister to the saints when the saints are dispersed, and when they're gone from the kinds of day-to-day interactions that we were accustomed to having pre-Covid? How does a shepherd lead the sheep when they're scattered across hill and valley and the sheepfold stands empty?

Oh, I know these sheep-and-shepherd metaphors are just that, metaphorical. And I know that buildings don't constitute the church, and that the people who comprise the church, unlike the church windows and doors, can't be "re-opened" since as congregants they were never "closed off" from being the people of God.

Nevertheless, I'm increasingly feeling the loss of our life together. Here we are, suddenly a diaspora people, having just built a large multi-purpose space in which to gather, but it now stands as empty as that ancient "sheepfold" after the crucifixion of Christ, when the apostles were scattered to the wind. Here we are, summarily exiled from common fellowship around the communion table. And here we are, a recently assembled and wonderfully effective ministry team of committed and spiritually sensitive leaders, most of whom are in their thirties, and all of whom have been benched.

Tonight I led our bi-weekly prayer meeting on Zoom, our newly consecrated sanctuary in the sky. After sharing and praying with the other four persons on the call, I realized how much better I felt for having been with them for a single hour. Even a postmodern Zoom session gave us a present sense of purpose, meaning, and hope. "For where two or three are gathered together in my name, I am there among them" (Matt 18:20), lest in our collective state of isolation we forget him.

Sociologists, who say things that most people have already been thinking, classify such things with fancy terms that sound more or less unique. One such obvious phenomenon they gave a textbook definition called "role theory."

Role theory simply means that each of us assumes various and sundry roles in life: employee or employer, parent or child, athlete or couch potato, spouse or partner, student or teacher, reader or writer, pastor or minister, priest or prophet, rabbi or imam, church member or country clubber, philanthropist or gambler, golf pro or panhandler. The list goes on.

Sociologists argue that such roles, obviously, are socially defined and constructed, lasting only so long as they have social utility. So, if a choir director loses the choir in a bus accident, then the choir director no longer has the role of choir director, at least for that choir. A shepherd cannot be a shepherd without sheep. Parents cannot be parents without children. A spouse cannot be a spouse apart from having a spouse. A professor needs students since, without them, to whom does a professor "profess"? In other words, when the actual relational function of a social role disappears, the role disappears.

Oh, we might still call ourselves by whatever name the role once had. Yet everything that came with the role fades away, including our role-defined personal identity, our role-associated emotions, and the expectations that others had of us when exercising the role. We are left with but a label with no existentially useful or meaningful purpose attached. What is a dogcatcher without a dog to catch, or a lover without a person to love? Over time, "role-evaporation" gets its own sociological nomenclature.

Yes, I find it truly difficult to be the pastor of a congregation without a flock. And that's not because the flock is nowhere to be found. It's simply because its whereabouts is beyond my immediate horizon. Over the hill, you could say, or lost in the woods. Or, more likely, hidden behind a computer screen, trying to figure out how to get into a Zoom session.

In the absence of what the French sociologist Emile Durkheim called "dynamic density," which is the positive energy that comes from rich social interactions found in religious settings, pastors are left mostly with fleeting memories and socially-distanced interactions with a few saints who phone from the other end of a city named "Deserted." For there is no good substitute for the "dynamic density" we draw from looking at one another, teary-eyed with arms outstretched, at the sounds of long-unseen children splitting the air with great laughter.

During this pandemic, teachers have lost sight of their students. Employees have lost sight of their colleagues. Children have lost sight of their schoolmates. And persons without work and a paycheck have fallen into the pit of despair. Gazing at one another from a distance of six feet and from behind a mask doesn't make for adequate "compensation." That's because we're social creatures to the very core of our being. When we're without socialization, we're like a knotty old tree with leafless limbs surrounded by nothing but desert. We need more than the whistling wind to know that we're still alive and breathing.

My friend told me this morning that, as he talks with other pastors, he is left wondering how many may simply resign from the pastorate in the middle of the pandemic. Caught in conflicts about how and if and when to reassemble their congregations, the stress hormones set in and curdle the flow of blood to the brain, to say nothing of the heart.

Throwing in the towel is always an option. But so are the words of Jesus: "Could you not stay awake with me one hour?" (Matt 26:40b). Perhaps, as on Easter morn, the women of the church will be the first to tell us (male pastors) that *he is alive*—and so are we!—since they seem to have a way of gaining entry to the disbelieving hearts of disciples when the stone of death is rolled away from the tomb of despair.

In a course on aging and spirituality that I developed at Elizabethtown College as the result of my Parkinson's diagnosis, and that I team-taught with my colleague, Dr. Tamera Humbert, chair of the occupational therapy department, it was thanks to her that she introduced me to a concept called "Theory U" that was developed by Otto Scharmer at MIT several decades ago.[27] Like many a

---

[27]   Otto Scharmer, *The Essentials of Theory U* (Oakland, CA: Berrett-Koehler, 2018). http://book.ottoscharmer.com/.

sociological concept, it is almost self-explanatory for its simplicity and usefulness.

The idea is that when a society or an organization enters a period of crisis, its path takes a downward turn toward the bottom of the U. And when we are the ones falling down into the U, it feels like all hell has broken loose. We lose our bearings, our footing, and our grounding. And, yes, we lose, in part if not entirely, the roles we played before we tripped off of the edge of the cliff.

After falling, we eventually find ourselves at the initial bend of the curve in the U, just before reaching bottom. It is at this bend that the journey suddenly becomes critical as to whether or not we will reach the tipping point from which to move up the other side of the U. For it is that other side, which for the moment we can't see, that represents the rebuilding, reconstruction, re-creation, and restoration of what, to put it in theological terms, Jesus promised will take place in the new heaven and the new earth. For that bend in the curve is where, perhaps for the first time, we come to grips with the fact that we have fallen and skinned up ourselves. During the downward slide we were so busy trying to survive that we expended every last bit of adrenaline.

So, now, you and I are sitting on the ledge that has caught us by the seat of our pants. And as we look up and back to what is forever gone, as well as farther down into what appears to be an interminable abyss, you and I would be the lone exceptions if we did not feel a rush of despair composed of grief and fear.

The problem for the pastor and anyone else perched on the ledge of the abyss is that there is no way to return to the way things were. Neither is there any glory to be had by cascading headlong into the chasm. To attempt to rest back into one's familiar role, whatever that was, which is now suspended, is only a delusional panacea. And preaching to the chasm may make a great noise but only because it echoes back and forth between the walls of oblivion, and not because "the sound and the fury" will in any way redeem us.

So, what do you do when you can't see your way forward? You can call out blindly into the darkness, of course. You can hope that somebody else somewhere, clinging to something more stable than the cotton in your jeans, hears you. And who might that be? And then what?

From where I currently sit on the ledge, I would never tell another pastor what to do. It would be unmercifully unkind of me. For the Lord only knows how often I've written a resignation letter inside my head over the past fifteen years. So, I get it when it comes to being dumbfounded about what to do next when I'm stymied at the edge of the ledge. Yet there is a question that another pastor once put to me. If you are in the midst of the desolation—maybe not the desolating sacrilege (Mark 13:14), but the momentary desolation—is that a good time to make the decision to leap into the dark?

For some, maybe, for others, maybe not. But if you can just hang on, there is a way, slight though it may seem, to see light that sheds clarity upon the situation. I'm thinking of Paul's words to the Christians at Corinth. "Therefore," he said, "since it is by God's mercy that we are engaged in this ministry, we do not lose heart" (2 Cor 4:1).

"Since it is *by God's mercy* that we are engaged."

That way of framing it offers me comfort and the necessary recognition. For the necessary recognition is that, although some days ministry feels like shoveling hot coals in hell, it's actually grace that's always gotten me to and through the tipping point, inching my way up the other side of the "U." "*By God's mercy*," I catch a glimmer of the kingdom to come. And a glimmer is all that I need.

But today, I must admit, I questioned whether Saint Paul was writing those words in the midst of a pandemic. Perhaps, if he could speak to me now, he would say, *Come on, Kanagy, what are you possibly thinking?*

> Three times I was beaten with rods. Once I received a stoning. Three times I was shipwrecked; for a night and a day I was adrift at sea; on frequent journeys, danger from bandits, danger from my own people, danger from Gentiles, danger in the city, danger in the wilderness, danger at sea, danger from false brothers and sisters; in toil and hardship, through many a sleepless night, hungry and thirsty, often without food, cold and naked. And, besides other things, I am under daily pressure because of my anxiety for all the churches. (2 Cor 11:25-28)

As I hear those words of litany from the labored heart of the steadfast apostle, the church bells clanging in my head are the Spirit's voice summoning me to keep on moving ahead.

CHAPTER TWENTY-SIX

Dear Church Member: What Shepherds See and What Some Sheep Do Not
September 2020

I know that with what I'm about to say I risk appearing self-serving, but keep in mind that I'm an old guy with Parkinson's disease and I'm not much of a threat to anyone. I've also been in ministry long enough to obtain tenure, which in higher education, at least, means I've earned the right to speak my mind on behalf of my colleagues who don't yet have permanent employment status.

Since my own sundown is within sight, these words are offered less on my own behalf than on behalf of those many pastors I know to be struggling, and wondering whether to stick with their calling as the sanction of God's mercy or as the indictment of God's curse.

One of my early research interests dates back to my graduate school days and was concerned with the differences between clergy and church members when it came to views of racism during this nation's Civil Rights era. The data were clear. Clergy overwhelmingly supported the Civil Rights Movement and concerted efforts to address racial injustice, more so than the persons sitting in the pews. This should not have come as much of a surprise.

Throughout biblical and subsequent church history, rich with literature containing metaphors of migratory people and animals, those whom God called to lead God's "flocks of sheep" typically saw the landscape from a different perspective than the ones they led. If that had not been the case, then shepherds would not have been shepherds. Instead, they would have been among the many ewes or rams wandering about, needing to be led. There is good reason as to why shepherds develop a different view of the field than the flocks that they lead.

Watchful shepherds lie awake at night, scanning the horizon while the flock is asleep. During daylight, shepherds are constantly mindful of the sheep that are in imminent danger of wandering away or being captured by predatory animals or thieving people. Good shepherds discern dangers lurking about, as well as locations where food and water may be found. More often than the sheep are aware, shepherds place themselves between their vulnerable flocks and the hungry wolves that seek to devour them. In doing so, they put their own lives and livelihoods in jeopardy. That is also true for the shepherds who faithfully lead the flocks of God's people.

Good shepherds are given a Christological view of the landscape that the Chief Shepherd provides them. "'Suppose one of you has only one sheep and it falls into a pit on the sabbath; will you not lay hold of it and lift if out? How much more valuable is a human being than a sheep!" (Matt 12:11–12a). Jesus said:

> "I am the good shepherd. The good shepherd lays down his life for the sheep. The hired hand, who is not the shepherd and does not own the sheep, sees the wolf coming and leaves the sheep and runs away—and the wolf snatches them and scatters them. The hired hand runs away because a hired hand does not care for the sheep. I am the good shepherd. I know my own and my own know me, just as the Father knows me and I know the Father. And I lay down my life for the sheep. I have other sheep that do not belong to this fold. I must bring them also, and they will listen to my voice." (John 10:11–16a)

A good shepherd seeks the welfare of all of the sheep. And this includes the sheep of other flocks that the ones presently being tended by the shepherd may not see as among their own. During the Civil Rights era, and in many respects as much today as then, when the shepherd reached out to those "other sheep that do not belong to this fold," the wolves that were dressed in sheep's clothing got restless and roamed about the flock, stirring up deep discontent.

Preaching the gospel sometimes offends. "Blessed is anyone who takes no offense at me," said our Lord (Matt 11:6). "The disciples approached and said to him, 'Do you know that the Pharisees took offense when they heard what you said?' He answered, 'Every plant that my heavenly Father has not planted will be uprooted. Let them alone; they are blind guides of the blind. And if one blind person guides another, both will fall into a pit'" (15:12–14).

Preaching the gospel to any congregation has its pitfalls. The foremost is the failure of the undershepherd (the pastor) to listen to what the Chief Shepherd says. For then the undershepherd is a blind guide pulling only God knows how many of the sheep into the pit with him, for having preached something other than the gospel of Jesus Christ.

From a sociological as well as theological perspective, shepherds and sheep have different roles to exercise with respect to their churches' ministries. Yet the most dangerous of pitfalls is the one whereby the shepherds corrupt their sheep by sanctioning predominant values of the culture that clearly conflict with the tenets of the gospel. This happens notably when certain princes and politicians, among others, promote lies upon lies, and then certain spiritual leaders fall in line to perpetuate the same lies. For then, in exchange for the idolatrous prognostications of false prophets, the shepherds forfeit the truth that Christ anointed them to preach. This is more than heresy. This is apostasy.

Moreover, preachers who peddle a "prosperity gospel" do not preach the New Testament gospel of Jesus Christ. By the verdict of Saint Peter's epistle, "They have hearts trained in greed" (2 Pet 2:14c). Jesus, himself one of the poor, warned the rich, "Woe to you who are rich, for you have received your consolation. Woe to you who are full now, for you will be hungry. Woe to you who are laughing now, for you will mourn and weep" (Luke 6:24–25).

Paul foresaw the danger of false prophets. He said to the elders of the church at Ephesus, "Keep watch over yourselves and over all the flock, of which the Holy Spirit has made you overseers, to shepherd the church of God that he obtained with the blood of his own Son. I know that after I have gone, savage wolves will come in among you, not sparing the flock. Some even from your own group will come distorting the truth in order to entice the disciples to follow them" (Acts 20:28–30).

But accepting Christ's call to preach the gospel can be akin to facing 100, 200, 300 or more employers, any one of whom may decide that last Sunday's sermon warranted firing the preacher, but for the wrong reason: because the preacher preached the gospel. And that same person who grouses about the affront of a prophetic sermon may be the very person who in a moment of personal crisis calls upon the preacher for urgent pastoral care, but then once the crisis has passed, shakes down the preacher again with a chastising email circulated throughout the congregation. Or even worse, confronts the preacher with a "word from the Lord" before they are barely out of the pulpit. It's so hard to argue with saints who've "heard from the Lord" during a sermon that their pastor prayed about and prayed for the week before.

When it comes to prophetic preaching about the collective sins of White supremacy, racism, homophobia, misogyny, and xenophobia, among other sins that the gospel of Christ's love condemns in order that they be confessed, Paul was nobody's fool. To reiterate what he said, "Some even from your own group will come distorting the truth in order to entice the disciples to follow them" (Acts 20:30). And Paul also said, "If I have all faith, so as to remove mountains, but do not have love, I am nothing" (1 Cor 13:2b).

Pastor and scholar Will Willimon has written: "Xenophobic, exclusionary fear of the Other is more than a matter of preference for people whom we enjoy hanging out with, or those with whom we feel most comfortable. In deep fear of the Other, we separate ourselves from others in order to better oppress, exploit, expulse, confine, hurt, or deny justice and access to others whom we have judged to be so Other as to be beyond the bounds of having any bond between us or any claim upon us."[28]

Such exclusionary fears and their accompanying actions, when seen through the eyes of Christ who deliberately breaks down the barriers that separate people and nations, signify egregious falsehoods about the "other." And, too often, for calling such sins precisely what they are, preachers get roasted and, along with Jesus and the Hebrew prophets, end up losing their jobs.

The sociologist Robert Bellah and his colleagues published in 1986 what is considered a classic study of American religion, entitled *Habits of the Heart*.[29] In it they interviewed a woman named Sheila Larson who identified her religion as "Sheilaism," which was her own religion related strictly to herself. As Sheila said, "I believe in God. I'm not a religious fanatic. I can't remember the last time I went to church. My faith has carried me a long way. It's Sheilaism. Just my own little voice."[30]

---

[28]   Will H. Willimon, *Fear of the Other* (Nashville: Abingdon Press, Kindle Edition, 2018), 14.
[29]   Robert Bellah et al, *Habits of the Heart: Individualism and Commitment in American* Life (New York: Harper & Row, Publishers, 1985.
[30]   *Habits of the Heart*, 221.

What Bellah and his cohorts illustrated was that Sheilaism represents a privatized form of religion that, even for those who do go to church, takes its cues from an entrenched secularism characterized by supersaturated "rugged individualism." That secular mindset produces churches that are "no longer made up of the whole community but only of the like-minded." Such churches are "not so much pillars of public order as 'protected and withdrawn islands of piety.'"[31]

Within the prevailing context of an "island-piety," the collective sins of society are quietly nurtured and perpetuated with implicit if not explicit religious blessing. Consequently, a prophet of the Christian gospel, who stands before a segregated White congregation (whether calling itself Evangelical or not), and who calls for a confession of the sins of White supremacy and racism, is sooner or later bound to encounter resistance if not outright renunciation. For it is at this point that "Sheilaism" has become "sheepism," as where in the book of Judges it says, "In those days there was no king in Israel; all the people did what was right in their own eyes" (Judg 21:25).

Is it fair to say that Christ's true shepherds are no less subject to disposal today than Jesus was when the congregation ran him out of the synagogue for preaching from a controversial text from the prophet Isaiah?

> "The Spirit of the Lord is upon me, because he has anointed me to bring good news to the poor. He has sent me to proclaim release to the captives and recovery of sight to the blind, to let the oppressed go free, to proclaim the year of the Lord's favor." (Luke 4:18–19)

Everything I'm hearing from pastors these days suggests that shepherd's work is a lonely and risky business. But until you've been

---

[31]   *Habits of the Heart*, 223.

there, out in front of the tumult and clamor, it's hard to comprehend just how lonely and risky this business is.

In my 2006–07 study of the American church, I surveyed both members and pastors. I discovered that pastors were more likely to talk about their faith to others than were lay persons. Such pastors were also more likely to invite people into the transformative presence of Christ where conversions take place, and more likely to invite non-Christians to Christian worship than were current church members. In other words, pastors were significantly more active evangelically than the persons in the pews.

At the same time, these pastors were more likely in their prophetic preaching to challenge the use of military might by the U.S. government than congregants were willing to do the same. And these pastors were more likely to oppose Christians participating in war, and more likely to support unified actions of non-violence.

In addition, when we asked lay members what they most wanted their pastors to do, they listed preaching first and pastoral care second. When we asked pastors for their priorities, they selected preaching, casting a vision for the congregation, and equipping the congregation to engage in ministry. Among most Protestant congregations there is usually agreement between pastor and people about placing preaching at the top of the to-do list, or at least until certain sermons are preached on sticky subjects.

So, dear church member, I thought I would set forth a few of these things for you to consider before you send the next email or text message to your pastor, or before you confront them just as they are leaving the pulpit, especially when you are seismically disgruntled about something he or she said from behind that pulpit. Because it's quite possible that some person you know in the congregation is on the phone (or soon will be) with your pastor, due to some deadly tragedy that has knocked at that person's door.

Or the person on the phone with your pastor is a loving parent whose child is gay and dreadfully fearful of coming out of the closet.

Or the person on the phone with your pastor wants to know what to do for the next-door neighbor who is an undocumented immigrant terrified at the prospect of being deported back to where her brother was mowed down by the drug cartel.

Or the person on the phone with your pastor is calling from the city jail for having been arrested at a Black Lives Matter demonstration and is without money for bail.

Or the person on the phone with your pastor is another local pastor whose spouse has just committed suicide.

Or the person on the phone is your pastor calling you to ask how you are doing, that is, how you are truly doing beneath the mask you must wear while working all day at the supermarket less than a week after you buried your husband who is now in the all-embracing arms of Jesus, having "passed" from death to life due to the ravaging fever of Covid, without your loving presence having been at his side.

So, dear church member. No, let's simply say, Dear One. For here's what Jesus would say to you or anyone—anyone—on the other end of the phone: "I am the good shepherd. I know my own and my own know me, just as the Father knows me and I know the Father. And I lay down my life for the sheep. I have other sheep that do not belong to this fold. I must bring them also, and they will listen to my voice" (John 10:14–16a).

CHAPTER TWENTY-SEVEN

The Problem with Prophets
March 2021

L et's begin with words we have already heard, for they are among the words of Jesus that need to be heard again and again. Jesus began his ministry by making clear just what he was up to.

> "The Spirit of the Lord is upon me, because he has anointed me to bring good news to the poor. He has sent me to proclaim release to the captives and recovery of sight to the blind, to let the oppressed go free, to proclaim the year of the Lord's favor." (Luke 4:18–19)

This is great news, unless, of course, you and I can't be counted among the poor, the imprisoned, the blind, the oppressed, and those slaves who are slated to be set free, come the year of Jubilee. The issue for us, then, is where exactly we fit into Jesus's redemptive project for the world. For we have sought so hard to be among those with social status, those who count themselves free, and those who seek to be honored, esteemed, and given recognition, that there doesn't appear there will be much space for us in God's coming kingdom. Consequently, it doesn't take long for us to start muttering.

"But isn't this just Joseph and Mary's boy? Didn't he grow up over there on Walnut Street? Wasn't he that strange one, always a little odd? Wasn't his father a meagre carpenter? And didn't his parents begin their marriage incriminated with scandal?"

Jesus quickly responds, "Truly I tell you, no prophet is accepted in the prophet's hometown" (4:24). But why is that so?

Because the hometown folks always have a way of domesticating the prophet, of keeping the prophet in the prophet's place, which is that socially designated space we've carved out exclusively for the prophet so that we don't have to occupy it as our space. For if the prophet begins to move into our space, then who knows what the prophet may require of us? Better that we drive him "out of town" and lead him to "the brow of the hill" and "hurl him off the cliff" (4:29).

But, of course, the true prophet has a way of passing through our midst and going his own way, which is God's way (4:30).

Sociologists note that social reality operates at two levels. There is the macro level of social institutions, such as economic structures, governmental complexes, criminal justice systems, health care systems, religious establishments, and public media. But these institutions also press down upon the micro level of families, neighborhoods, work places, and ultimately the individual person. The problem we have with hometown prophets is that they know our hometown territories all too well at both of these levels. So, whatever the local prophet says to us hometowners, we take it as personal affront, as criticism, as judgement, as condemnation. For when our neighbor Cecelia, Óscar, Rosa, Uchimura, or Martin steps over the line, well, it simply threatens the whole kit and caboodle, and we've already made plain we're not about to change, no matter what the prophet says.

Can you think of any on your home turf who are thoroughly committed to being obstinate obstructionists as soon as the prophet opens his mouth? Maybe it's downright true that the proper adjective for the establishment's obstructionists is "downwrong."

In a great book that Heidi and I read by Tod Bolsinger, entitled *Tempered Resilience: How Leaders Are Formed in the Crucible of*

Leaders Change Agents. Non

Change,[32] Bolsinger distinguishes managers from leaders. The church loves managers. The church also says it loves leaders until, well, until they begin to lead, since leadership requires change. And change means loss. For most of us loss is viewed as risky, dangerous, and unsafe. It's not long before we start looking for that hill from which to send the change-leader cascading down. Invariably, Bolsinger says, that leader is "sabotaged."

So, do we understand what we're saying when we declare Jesus, the prophet and change-leader, to be our Lord? That we're opening ourselves to uncertainty, just as Jesus did? To insecurity? To peril? To danger? To loss? Maybe even to death? Or have we domesticated Jesus to the point that he is entirely indistinguishable from the money merchant down the street who says to the customer, "Bank your money here because you'll never lose a single dime"? But then Jesus responds, "For those who want to save their life will lose it, and those who lose their life for my sake, and for the sake of the gospel, will save it" (Mark 8:35).

I have long loved the prayer by the 19th century Scottish writer, George MacDonald.

> For thou art making me, I thank thee, sire.
> What thou hast done and doest thou know'st well,
> And I will help thee: gently in thy fire
> I will lie burning; on thy potter's wheel
> I will whirl patient, though my brain should reel.
> Thy grace shall be enough the grief to quell,
> And growing strength perfect through weakness dire.[33]

---

[32]   Tod Bolsinger, *Tempered Resilience: How Leaders Are Formed in the Crucible of Change* (Downers Grove: InterVarsity Press, 2020).

[33]   George MacDonald, "But thou art making me, I thank thee, sire," October 2, *Diary of an Old Soul* (Minneapolis: Augsburg Publishing House, 1975), 101. Public domain.

George MacDonald's is a prophet's prayer. Molded on the Potter's wheel, refined in the Potter's fire, the prophet knows his own weakness when standing before those who would strike him down, knows that the only way forward is to know the God before whom he is malleable, by whom he is shaped into the person whose strength God alone provides in the midst of the whirlwind and the fiery ordeal.

"Nobody knows the trouble I see, Nobody knows my sorrow; Nobody knows the trouble I see, Glory, hallelujah!"[34]

What is the trouble, the trial, the biblical prophet sees? Walter Brueggemann, Old Testament teacher, Hebraic scholar, and author of *The Prophetic Imagination*,[35] frames the contextual situation—the trouble, the trial—posed for the prophet of God, be it Moses, Jeremiah, Jesus, or any modern-day prophet. The trial-and-trouble frame is that of "the royal consciousness" which defines the prevailing ethos of an entire population, be it the land of Egypt under the Pharaohs, the United Kingdom of Israel under Solomon, or the city of Jerusalem under the Roman Caesar Tiberius. "It takes little imagination to see ourselves in this same royal tradition," states Brueggemann.

Ourselves in an economics of affluence in which we are so well off that pain is not noticed and we can eat our way around it.

Ourselves in a politics of oppression in which the cries of the marginal are not heard or are dismissed as the noises of kooks and traitors.

Ourselves in a religion of immanence and accessibility, in which God is so present to us that his abrasiveness, his absence, his banishment are not noticed, and the problem is reduced to psychology.[36]

---

[34] Traditional Negro spiritual.

[35] Walter Brueggemann, *The Prophetic Imagination* (Minneapolis: Fortress Press, 1978).

[36] *The Prophetic Imagination*, 41.

"Perhaps you are like me," says Brueggemann,

> so enmeshed in this reality that another way is nearly un-
> thinkable. The dominant history of that [biblical] period, like
> the dominant history of our own time, consists in briefcases
> and limousines and press conferences and quotas and new
> weaponry systems. And that is not a place where much *dancing*
> happens and where no *groaning* is permitted.[37]

Nevertheless, the prophet comes along *dancing and groaning*
before God. The prophet's God is "uncredentialed in the empire,
unknown in the courts, unwelcome in the temple. And his history
[God's history] begins in his attentiveness to the cries of the marginal ones. He [God], unlike his royal agents, is one whose person
is presented as passion and pathos, the power to care, the capacity
to weep, the energy to grieve and then to rejoice. The prophets after
Moses know that his caring, weeping, grieving, and rejoicing will not
be outflanked by royal hardware or royal immunity because this one
is indeed God. And kings must face that."[38]

And so must the hometown folks. Because God through the
prophet has something to say to us. God's prophet is given the prophetic imagination and zeal with which to mobilize the people to do
what God calls the people to do even when the "royal consciousness"
is determined to defy God every step of the way.

If only we recognize that the prophet speaks God's truth and
not falsehood, then we are set free.

If only we recognize how sick we are, then the prophet calls
upon God to heal us.

If only we recognize that the merciful justice of the living and

---

37   *The Prophetic Imagination*, 41–42.
38   *The Prophetic Imagination*, 42.

loving God carries to the ends of the earth, then the prophet's word removes the shackles from our ankles so that we may join in the dance.

"Dance, then, wherever you may be; I am the Lord of the Dance, said He. And I'll lead you all wherever you may be, and I'll lead you all in the dance, said He."[39]

---

[39]   Nineteenth century Shaker hymn, words by Sydney Carter, 1963. With permission.

PART SIX

A DISMANTLED BODY
IN A CHURCH DISMANTLED

CHAPTER TWENTY-EIGHT

Parkinson's Disease, the Gifts of Dying Churches, and the Glory to Come

May 2021

I n one of my favorite passages of scripture, Saint Paul sets his eyes clearly on what is unseen beyond what is seen. He declares that because God has raised Jesus from the dead, we too shall be raised to new life with Jesus, and that it is God "who has shone in our hearts to give the light of the knowledge of the glory of God in the face of Jesus Christ" (2 Cor 4:6).

> We have this treasure in clay jars so that it may be made clear that this extraordinary power belongs to God and does not come from us. We are afflicted in every way, but not crushed; perplexed, but not driven to despair; persecuted, but not forsaken; struck down, but not destroyed; always carrying in the body the death of Jesus, so that the life of Jesus may also be made visible in our bodies. . . . Death is at work in us, but life in you. . . . So we do not lose heart. Even though our outer nature is wasting away, our inner nature is being renewed day by day. For this slight momentary affliction is preparing us for an eternal weight of glory beyond all measure, because we look not at what can be seen but at what cannot be seen; for what can be seen is temporary, but what cannot be seen is eternal. (vv. 7–18)

So, what then are we to make of the death that is at work in us, yet also the life of Jesus that is visible in us?

I must confess that as both a sociologist of religion and a follower of Jesus, I have long assumed that the European churches, Anabaptist and otherwise, are at the tail end of a death-procession of the saints, disappearing into the surrounding secular society and culture. At the same time, the churches within the United States and the global South seem to have possessed greater vitality.

However, after reading "Walking on Water" by Henk Stenvers, a leader of the Mennonite Church in the Netherlands,[40] I recognize that I had failed to appreciate what the Spirit was up to among the European churches, and what this can teach the rest of us. Let us give the Dutch Mennonite Church credit for being around longer than the rest of the Anabaptist communities, adding, as well, the Swiss movement of Mennonites to the short list of long-haulers.

Let us also say that it's somewhat arrogant for the rest of us among the western Christian churches to assume that, by the time our Anabaptist communities reach their 500th birthday, we will be in any better position than our European brothers and sisters. In fact, I'm confident that the North American churches are now much closer to the experience of our European cousins than I had thought to be the case even in the recent past.

The difference may be that we in the United States have found effective ways to deny the fact that Christian congregations are dying. Sociologists speak of the American churches in terms of their comprising an ecclesiological marketplace, with church-shopping and church-switching making it easier for people eventually to bail out of churches altogether.

Like those large shopping malls and "big box" stores across the landscape that caused the demise of "mom and pop" shops on Amer-

---

[40]   Henk Stenvers, "Walking on Water," Part 1, "Concerning the Future of the Dutch Mennonites" (Algemene Doopsgezinde Societëit), Feb. 3, 2021. https://achurchdismantled.com/henk-stenvers-essay/. With permission.

ica's Main Streets, we in ecclesiastical circles have been busily building megachurches with their smorgasbords of programs that have led to the death of small community congregations. And now, as Amazon, eBay, and other Internet giants swamp the planet with an unprecedented geo-commercialism, forcing large-scale malls and department stores into bankruptcy, so too we Christians must consider the ramifications of commodifying the churches, or what we could aptly label the "McDonaldization"[41] of American religion "on my terms," "at my convenience," and "customized to my individual preferences."

There is, however, no evidence to suggest that megachurches increase overall church attendance in the United States. To the contrary, there are indications that megachurches have reduced the sense and importance of what it means for churches to be integral communities of Christ's disciples.

As with most pastors, I am bombarded with emails from so-called "ministries" that promise the next and best answer for whatever happens to ail or afflict our local congregation at the moment, with the assurance of resuscitating our last dying breath. It seems that the incentive to capitalize profits by marketing the most recent ecclesiastical contraptions to churches amounts to little more than gimmickry promoted to save churches from being trapped in a death-spiral.

This is why I and others have found the words of people like Henk Stenvers, a theologian of the Netherlands, to be so comforting. For he believes it is time to let go of what was, to release our dying churches to God, and to trust that the resurrection of Jesus Christ remains the singular truth upon which we must rely, in contrast to our own ingenuity. In other words, let the Spirit be the guiding Spirit of the churches.

Let's acknowledge that all seven of the churches in the book of Revelation also met their dying day, having disappeared within

---

[41]   George Ritzer, *The McDonaldization of Society: Into the Digital Age*, 9th ed. (Thousand Oaks: Sage Publishers, 2018).

the prevailing secularity and population swings of Asia Minor as well as the rising tide of Islam. But this fact does not diminish their trans-historical influence, nor does it negate the reality that true and obedient followers of Jesus once constituted those churches. I hold to the belief that the prayers offered by those saints continue to be effectual throughout God's eternity. By the same token, we today are no more immune to the ecclesial comings-and-goings of our age than they were long ago to theirs. Nor should we think for a moment that our prayers will be of no avail for generations of saints to come after us. For it is the Spirit who prays within us and the Spirit who transmits our prayers wherever the Spirit wills.

Perhaps my perspective on this is most impacted by recognizing that, due to my diagnosis of Parkinson's disease four years ago, I, too, am diminishing as I prematurely age. No amount of pecuniary bargaining for the latest ministry-gimmick is going to change that fact. Consequently, I find myself viewing the horizon as would someone who is fifteen to twenty years my senior. Rather than spinning my energy in a flight of denial, I have chosen to embrace a foreshortened view of my life and recognize that there are some things I must release. One of them is my role as a lead pastor, a decision I would not have anticipated apart from my diagnosis. The reality of Parkinson's has foreclosed the fulfillment of my earlier dream to carry on at least another ten years. Yet, as I have previously said, facing this limitation head-on has enabled me to find a new purpose consistent with the life I must now live. As a result, I am far more content and peaceful than were I to remain in a state of denial. It is a peacefulness gleaned from the words of Henk Stenvers.

> Let us relinquish what is keeping us from heading out. It
> is better to be a community of people who choose for God and
> people en route, than a community of people who try to cling

to what they have but consequently lose Jesus, God, the other, and ultimately themselves. . . . When Jesus is in our boat, when Jesus is present in the people in our group, we experience the world as less threatening, and the storm in us dies down, too. We can then go on courageously. . . . Going new ways is only possible if we relinquish the fear of an unknown future and focus on what we are good at in the congregation. In this way, congregations can be attractive groups to which people belong. To be a genuine faith community, and remain one, we need to return to the content of our faith and place priority on the imitation of Jesus.[42]

A couple of years after my diagnosis, I told our congregation that I had experienced a new conversion to Jesus and a new aware-ness of the love of God for me. But I do not believe this would have occurred without acknowledging that I am living on God's gifted time, which from my perspective seems to be borrowed time. But as Henk affirmed, how much better to choose for God, no matter the circumstances that bring us to this point, rather than forego the gain we have in Jesus's resurrection by seeking to cling to what inevitably we must lose of ourselves in the present moment.

Since for a long time it seemed to me that we of the West-ern churches were chiefly devoid of spiritual vitality, I used to think that our financial resources were the greatest gift we had to offer the global church. But I see that differently now. At this moment in particular, the churches of Europe offer the global church, in-cluding churches in the United States, ways to let go of everything that detracts from our being faithful emissaries of Jesus Christ in a changing and troubled world. The European churches show us that losing our grip on current systems, infrastructures, and programs can

---

42   "Walking on Water," 37–38.

actually free us to become the church that God is shaping us to be, however indiscernible the church of tomorrow may be today. For as the apostle Paul said about his own confidence for the future, "What can be seen is temporary, but what cannot be seen is eternal."

Our sixteen-year-old Cocker Spaniel, Buffy, needs to make one last visit to the vet to be released from her pain and her somewhat demented state. I've already made two appointments and cancelled both. I've had to ask myself whether I'm unwilling to let go of her for reasons of my own selfishness or for reasons related to her well-being. I've concluded that it's mainly for my own sake that I've been reluctant to release her to the loving embrace of God.

So, I ask myself, what does it take for us Christians to release the church to the loving embrace of Jesus? To be converted anew to the power of Jesus's resurrection at work here and now among us? To relinquish what is peripheral to our purpose for the sake of what is central to God's purpose?

What does it take for us to let God be God? To let God lower the mountains and raise the valleys, to set straight the crooked places and make smooth the rough places—including all of those within God's Church? Jesus calls us to be salt and light in the world, which is to say, to *be* God's church.

"We have this treasure in clay jars, so that it may be made clear that this extraordinary power belongs to God and does not come from us" (2 Cor 4:7).

CHAPTER TWENTY-NINE

It's as if Everyone Has Parkinson's Disease

May 2020

Over the past two months, I have found myself saying that "it's as if everyone has Parkinson's disease." When I was diagnosed on February 14, 2017 (Happy Valentine's Day!), the physician at Penn University Hospital informed me this way: "There is no alternative diagnosis."

Apparently, that was her less than sensitive way of beating around the bush about the diagnosis, and how I might feel about receiving the bad news. For a physician it was less than desirable bedside manner. I just wanted to know the truth. After informing me, she simply dismissed us and scheduled an appointment for two months out. On the next visit, following a physical exam, she repeated her same mantra: "There is no alternative diagnosis."

By this point, I had had some time to consider the possible consequence of "no alternative diagnosis," which to me was not encouraging. My family physician was even blunter: "You don't want to have that diagnosis; it is an all-encompassing disease" (as if I had a choice in the matter). Once again, whatever happened to the physician's bedside manner? I had also heard other observations that were hardly encouraging, like: "You will have a honeymoon period once you get on meds, but that period will come to an end." And: "Today you feel as good as you'll ever feel again in your entire life."

During my first year of living with the diagnosis, I cried and raged. The second year, I found a group of friends at Rock Steady Boxing who helped me normalize the new reality, as I began to accept the deck of cards I had been dealt. But by the third year, I heard myself saying, "When God gave me Parkinson's . . . ." And, to my surprise, I realized that I had said this with a matter-of-factness, void of pain and tears and rage (not that they had entirely disappeared). And also during the third year, I began to see that God had given me a gift—the gift of brokenness, the gift of an uncertain future—and yet, even so, the gift of a foreshortened horizon that I'd never been aware of before.

The gift of living with uncertainty is the recognition that uncertainty is our universal lot. For me, awareness of a limited horizon means seeing more clearly the things I've taken for granted all along, and being less prone to hide my anxieties, which, of course, my tremors have a way of instantly revealing.

The sum of these gifts is that I'm more grateful today than I was four years ago—for what God has given me. My students now identify with me as a human being rather than as a guy with a doctoral degree. And I'm freer than ever to be and say and do what I sense God is calling me to be and say and do. I've asked myself on many occasions, "What do I have to lose now?" With diminished anxiety, I have a new sense of purpose and perspective, a new freedom and joy.

So, what when our churches—the people, not the buildings— have been dealt a deck of cards similar to the one I was dealt? And that collectively we are burdened with a sense of chronic anxiety, or in some instances, hopelessness? Yet, we manage nevertheless to cover up our distress by dressing up as our "Sunday selves" for Sabbath worship, only to return to our "Monday-through-Saturday selves," spiritually in tatters and with our witness for Christ languishing in the shadows. We make a temporary peace with the incongruity that exists as a division between our two different selves, and signal as much when with the wink of an eye we pass one another in the pews.

Like anyone caught in the grip of grief after the shock of receiving the diagnosis of an incurable illness, we cry, we rage, and we try every possible way to return to the way things were before the diagnosis. We say to ourselves: *Surely, somehow, there must be a more favorable outcome. Maybe if we exercise more? Rage more? Rant more? Resist more? Then magically the shattered pieces of our life will all fit back together?*

On the other hand, what if we accept the truth of the diagnosis rather than deny it? What if we turn to God and say, *Lord, we may not understand, but we do accept. We accept that our spiritual disease is more than we alone can handle, and more than we alone have power to cure. Though far beyond our capacity to comprehend, as to why, or how, or exactly what comes next, we nonetheless receive this debilitating illness as somehow beneficial for us, and in that sense a holy gift. So we ask that you turn it to our advantage, and to the blessing of others as well. May your will be done on earth, in us, as it is in your heavenly kingdom.*

Might moving from resistance to acceptance, through prayer, alter the way we live and die from this point on? By dropping our "masked selves," might our eyes open to God's unfolding horizon, presenting us with a new purpose, a new freedom, a new courage, and an unspeakably new joy? Could ingesting yet another dose of the "Four Spiritual Laws" ever be anything other than a poor substitute for the medicinal powers of the Great Physician who listens to our prayers, and who hears our deepest anguish and fears?

So, we pray. And we do so just as he did. When facing his own final horizon, he "went, as was his custom, to the Mount of Olives, and the disciples followed him." There he "withdrew from them about a stone's throw, knelt down, and prayed, 'Father, if you are willing, remove this cup from me; yet, not my will but yours be done" (Luke 22:39, 41–42).

It's worth noting that when he withdrew, it was not to the temple with its crowds milling about the court of the Gentiles and the court of the Jews, but rather to that *place away* where "an angel from heaven appeared to him and gave him strength" (v. 43).

There are many such *places away* serving as sanctuaries of prayer for suffering souls seeking strength and hope in the presence of an angel.

As for me, by God's grace, one day an angel appeared. She said that she would walk with me, that Heidi and I would not be alone, and that with every change in my symptoms she would be there to guide me. Her name was Dr. Xuemei Huang of the Hershey Medical Center.

At the very last, with his eleven disciples standing at the mountain to which he "had directed them" in Galilee, "Jesus came and said to them . . . 'Remember, I am with you always, to the end of the age'" (Matt 28:20b).

Lord, now, and at the very last, we may not understand, but we do accept.

CHAPTER THIRTY

Boxing in Church
May 2020

As a little kid, I went one day with Mom to Grants Department Store in Burnham, PA, only to discover on the display shelf a television set. Having grown up to that point without TV, it may have been the first one I'd seen except for the day my Uncle Joe and Aunt Shirley rented one so that the entire Renno family could watch the moon landing. More than remembering the first persons who arrived on the moon, I remember that TV.

Its live screen featured a boxing match. I watched guys in gloves eyeing one another and—boom! boom! boom!—knock one another around. For some strange and inexplicable reason, I walked over to my mother and said, "Look Mom! Let me show you what those guys were doing." Promptly I held my fists to the air to show Mom just how hard I could hit. The trouble was that I had landed a punch right onto Mom!

Usually a tolerant person, she informed me then and there that boxing one's parent was not appropriate and that I would experience the necessary regret when we got home. I waited with more than a little suspense.

Needless to say, after that episode I never went back to boxing and never had any desire to do so. That is, not until about a year into my diagnosis of Parkinson's, when I heard about Rock Steady Boxing (RSB) as a program designed to address the degenerative features of Parkinson's. I stalled for a while but finally made contact with Sue

Ludwig who directed the program in Lancaster, PA. She invited me to visit Rock Steady Boxing for a workout some morning and see how things went.

I got to the Emerald Center about 6:30 a.m. in the dark. I walked nervously up to the door, like someone showing up to church for the first time. I rang the buzzer and waited. The person answering asked me, "Are you one us?" I assumed he meant, are you broken like we are, do you tremor as we do, do your muscles stiffen up like ours? I said yes, and he invited me in.

On the inside I was greeted with a question. "Will you be on our team this morning?" Ninety minutes later as I was leaving, someone yelled to me, "Will we see you next week?"

I've thought a lot about those questions in relation to being the servants of Christ. What if we were to ask similar questions of every stranger who showed up at the church door?

Are you one of us (meaning, are you as good as we are?) and do you smell as nice as we do? Are you dressed properly for church? Do you cover up your true self just as we do? Or, instead: Are you as broken as we are? Do you tremor with anxiety as we do? Do you feel shame for the same reasons we do? Do you have doubts like our doubts about God? Do you struggle as much as we struggle with self-acceptance? Are you in need of healing as we are? And if the answer to these is "yes," then say, "Come on in here and be one of us!"

When our visitors walk through the door and into the church, could we then ask them "will you join our team?" And, after the service is over and before they take leave of us, how about "will we see you next week?"

Consider the paradigm shift these three questions pose for the church: *Are you one of us? Will you join our team? Will we see you next week?* (Instead of only "thanks for coming.")

When I arrived home from my first go at Rock Steady Boxing,

Heidi asked how it went. I replied that it was a good morning and that I felt welcomed. But the thought of folks with Parkinson's being five, ten, and fifteen years older than I, which was haunting, I simply said I could not go back. Heidi strongly encouraged me to reconsider. And I did. In doing so, I found a community unlike any that I'd ever experienced. For I have been accepted by these Rock Steady Boxers "just as I am," being part of the team each morning "just as they are," as we look forward to seeing one another week after week.

We rarely talk about our disease. Instead, it's about our grandchildren, our vacations, our work lives, and yes, our disappointments, pain, discouragement, and more. Every first Monday of the month, Gerald, a retired pilot, organizes breakfast at the Olde Hickory Restaurant. Although he doesn't attend church himself, he always asks one of us "of the cloth" to lead the saying of grace before we eat. In the second year of my disease, my Rock Steady Boxing friends accepted me "just as I am" and helped me do the same for myself.

Eventually I dropped out of RSB for a few months, thinking I could do this stuff on my own. But truthfully, I couldn't. For without those friends to accept me "just as I am," which meant "just as I was," I ended up with a difficult semester at the college. In fact, several of them showed up at church, looking for me. And when "Rock Steady" Doug showed up one day, that was all I needed to pick up my "Rock Steady" gloves again.

That prompts me to ask a question of us at the church: With our gloves *off*, could we not do at least as well as the Rock Steady Boxers with their gloves *on*—when "just as I am" meets "just as you are"?

CHAPTER THIRTY-ONE

Fallen Tree, Chihuly Blown Glass, and a Dear Friend to Help Me Get Home

June 2020

On February 14, 2017, I heard those same words again at the University of Penn Medical Center regarding the Parkinson's tremors I had experienced.

"I don't think there is an alternative diagnosis"—which was no more than a reiteration of what I'd heard from my family physician when he said, *"Boy, you sure don't want to have this disease—it's all encompassing."*

Neither statement offered much hope. I quickly discovered that viewing my situation from the standpoint of medical science offered me little to no *ultimate* hope.

Before I learned of my diagnosis, by God's grace the congregation granted me a three-month sabbatical, which we were to embark upon later that summer. It was a providential gift. It allowed Heidi and me time to process together the excruciatingly painful and discouraging news we had received. It also spared us of the glare of earnest questioners until we first had a chance to listen deeply to God. And, as is so often the case, God's words for us came from a variety of unexpected sources.

The first was from a visit to the Chihuly Garden and Glass exhibit in Seattle, Washington. If you've ever seen the work of artist Dale Chihuly, then you'll understand why any attempt of mine to describe it can't begin to express the grand mystery and beauty of it all. What intrigued me most was that part of the exhibit which described Chihuly's change of artistic expression due to the onset of his disability.

"After losing sight in his left eye and dislocating his shoulder," the description stated, "Chihuly relinquished the gaffer (the 'boss') position and began drawing as a way to communicate his vision and designs to his team. The drawings evolved beyond a communication tool to become an important part of his expression." Chihuly later concluded, "Drawing really helps me to think about things. I am able to draw and work with a lot of color, and that inspires me."

Here was the first hint that my own dark, all-encompassing life-sentence to Parkinson's disease could be an opening to a new creativity and joy, to a new way of revealing to others what lay dormant within me.

It was by his giving up of the "gaffer" position that Chihuly's students were empowered to do what he had done so well. For it was by picking up his brush that Chihuly revealed to others the vision he saw for himself. Up to that point, all that folk could see of the artist was the grandeur and beauty of his art. But now, enabled by an awareness of Chihuly's disability, they could see into the heart and soul of the man, from whom the grandeur and beauty emerged. Dale Chihuly's disability had provided the big leap into his maturation as an artist and a mentor. It is no surprise, then, that his drawings now sell for thousands of dollars.

The second window of divine opening to my "Parkinson's self" came during our trip to the Olympic National Forest, which displayed a mystic beauty eliciting considerable awe.

As we hiked the trail, taking photos of gigantic trees standing in majestic splendor as they had for centuries, there appeared a lone one that I would not have noticed, except for the fact that it had fallen partway across the trail, but remained about eight feet above the path. Despite its misfortune, it had bent itself upward toward the infinite sky. It was that tree, among the other grand, straight, and upright ones surrounding, that caught my eye. I beheld it, not for its perfection but for its persistence—living, breathing, and rising in its crooked, twisted form—persevering against daunting odds, revealing an unparalleled beauty all its own.

It happened just then. As I stood before that arched inhabitant of the forest, I sensed myself more present to my life than I had ever been before. Perhaps, I thought, my own disability would now render me more useful than I could possibly imagine. By God's inscrutable providence that hobbled tree may have been positioned this way for decades. Who knows? And perhaps for the singular purpose that all passers-by, lame or laden with burdens, might trace its visage aloft, drawing light and strength from heaven above.

Finally, yet another divine opening during our trip, appeared in a passage from a book about Sabbath rest. It helped me realize that the disease of Parkinson's would make me considerably dependent upon others, more so than I was ever willing to be in the past. I began to see that the gift of dependency could be one of the greatest gifts I could receive, or for that matter offer in return. For God didn't create us to live independently of one another, nor independently of God himself. Why is it, then, that we think we can go it alone as if we must prove to ourselves, yet certainly not to God, that somehow our independence makes us invulnerable and invincible?

Wayne Cordeiro, in *Leading on Empty*, notes this truth: "When we wrestle with our own infirmities, we are not disqualified from God's plan for our lives. It may just mean we will arrive at it differently from the way we had intended. We may arrive leaning on the arm of a friend."[43]

---

[43]   Wayne Cordeiro, *Leading on Empty* (Bloomington, MN: Bethany House Publishers, 2009), electronic edition, 155.

For me, that thought hurled light into my darkness, causing me to view Heidi, my dear wife, in a way I had not seen her before. With my Parkinson's disease, I would need Heidi more than anyone else, in order to find my way home. And that recognition alone deepened my love and thanksgiving for the extraordinary gift that she is to me.

I needn't pretend anymore ~~that I could go it~~ alone. The mask of my independence had fallen away. The façade of my self-sufficiency had fissured and snapped like a dead limb breaking away from an aging tree. I had come to experience what Paul, that Jewish-Christian mystic and ambassador to the Gentiles, so eloquently wrote to the church at Corinth. It is worth our hearing Paul say it again.

> But we have this treasure in clay jars, so that it may be made clear that this extraordinary power belongs to God and does not come from us. We are afflicted in every way, but not crushed; perplexed, but not driven to despair; persecuted, but not forsaken; struck down, but not destroyed; always carrying in the body the death of Jesus, so that the life of Jesus may also be made visible in our bodies. (2 Cor 4:7–10)

Somehow, by the mystery of God revealed in Jesus Christ our Lord, the depth of our inner darkness disperses when encountering the brilliance of his light, even as the unveiling of our weakness reveals the abundance of his strength.

As Paul professed, "This slight momentary affliction is preparing us for an eternal weight of glory beyond measure" (v. 17).

So, if by chance I'm ever that Parkinson's man you see hobbling along the sidewalk, crouched over with age, with creases in my face, with shuffling feet, with cane in hand and a limp in my gait, then may you remember to see me just as I saw that fallen tree—bent over, to be sure—but turned upward, yes, yes—by the Light.

CHAPTER THIRTY-TWO

Jeffrey Long — focusing on mortality [handwritten]
ENRicher [...] spirituality [handwritten]

With at Least One Eye
on Our Dying Day
May 2020

I have a Hindu friend and colleague, Dr. Jeffrey Long, who teaches Asian religions. He recently was a guest lecturer in my course on aging and spirituality. He made the comment that those who focus on the day of their death tend to have a deeper and richer spirituality.

When I was a kid, I was intrigued with cemeteries. They connected me to the past. I wondered about the lives of those buried six feet under, now long forgotten by most. And I wondered about my own death. I wondered about what lay ahead of me between now and then.

There is a lovely old cemetery on the west side of Big Valley along a meandering stream, shaded with trees on its southwestern side. The remains of Revolutionary War and Civil War veterans rest in this particularly idyllic spot, where there is also the gravesite of a woman from the late nineteenth century.

Her life is commemorated with a beautiful tombstone consisting of a slate slab containing an intricate design of calligraphy with a Victorian look. Yet it is the "sermon" written upon the slate that caught my attention and that I've never forgotten. "Stranger as you pass me by, as you are now so once was I. / I as I am now so shall you be, therefore prepare to follow me."

I know nothing about the woman, except that in her death she left us words we do well to remember during this Covid crisis and beyond. The scripture is replete with verses similar to hers, such as this one from the psalmist: "For he knows how we were made; he remembers that we are dust. As for mortals, their days are like grass; they flourish like a flower of the field, for the wind passes over it, and it is gone, and its place knows it no more" (Ps 103:14–16).

Why do you suppose that, speaking through the psalmist, God is so mindful of our death as to keep its certainty so graphically before us, invisible though it is?

First, it is likely because we resist contemplating it ourselves. And secondly, because doing so can realign our compass heavenward instead of exclusively pointing it to something closer at hand. Yes, it is true that keeping one eye focused upon the day of our death can alter the way we navigate our course through life. For when heaven lays its not-so-distant promises and obligations upon us in anticipation of the coming splendor, we tend to attune ourselves better to the paths that God has set before us right here on earth. With our death partly in view we are able to gain an alternate perspective from which to deal with the ups and downs we are bound to encounter in the hours or weeks or years ahead.

What is so clear from the Bible is that the saints keep their eyes fixed upon something larger and far more glorious than the hardships and tragedies they may experience in the present moment. Regarding those martyrs of Israel who persevered in the faith, the author of the book of Hebrews puts it like this. Some "were tortured, refusing to accept release, in order to obtain a better resurrection. Others suffered mocking and flogging, and even chains and imprisonment. They were stoned to death, they were sawn in two, they were killed by the sword; they went about in skins of sheep and goats, destitute, persecuted, tormented—of whom the world was not worthy. They wandered in deserts and mountains, and in caves and holes in the ground" (Heb 11:35b–38). Is it fair to say, then, that they did not feel themselves to be exactly at home?

As a kid, those words—"of whom the world was not worthy"—which were about being tortured, mocked, and flogged, chained and imprisoned, stoned to death and sawn in two, gave me goose bumps. Was *that* how one was to become numbered among such a distinguished crowd?

The author of Hebrews says plainly, "all of these died in faith without having received the promises, but *from a distance they saw and greeted it*" (v. 12, emphasis mine). For that is the key. They had their sight fixed upon what they could not see right in front of them. "They confessed that they were strangers and foreigners on the earth, for people who speak in this way make it clear that they are seeking a homeland . . . a better country, that is, a heavenly one. Therefore God is not ashamed to be called their God; indeed, he has prepared a city for them" (vv. 13b–16).

I once had a good friend, a medical doctor, who couldn't understand why we Christians, of all people, could be so focused on sustaining our lives at all cost regardless of our present quality of life—as if we were somehow among those without hope. For if it is time to go to a better home, then why would we want to settle for a lesser one?

To long for that better country is not a death wish. It is a life wish. It is a desire to live where we were created originally to be, within the providence of God's new Eden after being cast out of the old one. Such yearning sets the compass toward that city that is already prepared for us, where there is neither death nor dying.

I recognize that there are tragic and untimely deaths, as well as naturally expected ones, when mourning the loss of persons we love so dearly exceeds our capacity to go on living without them. Were that not so, then our love for them would already have proven itself seriously diminished. At the same time, whenever I hear of an old saint's death being "terribly sad news," I can only wonder how diminished our theology of heaven is when it's actually time now to begin the partying!

I've often prayed that in the final moments of my life I shall be able to breathe a sigh of relief, and to thank God that I'm shortly to reach my eternal destination. Is that because I long for death? Or because I wish to leave behind those I so dearly love? Not at all. It's because I long for that better country and believe with all my heart that it is prepared for me and awaiting my arrival.

"They confessed that they were strangers and foreigners on the earth, for people who speak in this way make it clear that they are seeking a homeland . . . a heavenly one."

For that reason, I keep one eye on it, and sometimes two.

CHAPTER THIRTY-THREE

A Year of Dismantling, "The Last Children of Down Syndrome," and "Whatever You Do, Don't Allow Parkinson's Disease to Define You!"

December 2020

The year 2020 has been a year of dismantling at so many levels, including the further dismantling of the American church, producing greater uncertainty for local congregations about their future, added to a dismantling of democratic institutions once taken for granted, a dismantling of Hollywood movie sets, Broadway musicals, and collegiate and professional sports, along with a renewed effort to dismantle deep-seated racism and injustices of the criminal justice system in response to the killings of George Floyd and other Black citizens.

The instinct remains, however, to resist the dismantling of certain things that we may prefer to retain as they are, even to are our detriment. An example appeared in the cover story of the November 2020 issue of *The Atlantic*, entitled "The Last Children of Down Syndrome."[44] It is a disconcerting exposé, no matter what one's view may be of fetal genetic testing, abortion, and difficult ethical considerations surrounding treatments for congenital disabilities. The article presents the country of Denmark as exhibit number one of how to go about eliminating a dreaded disability from an entire pop-

---

[44] Sarah Zhang, "The Last Children of Down Syndrome," *The Atlantic*, November 2020, https://cdn.theatlantic.com/assets/media/magazine/pdfs/202012.pdf/.

ulation. In Denmark, nearly all expectant mothers are screened for fetal Down syndrome. Ninety-five percent of those who test positive elect abortion.

The author is neither judgmental nor inclined to express her own values. Yet she asks haunting questions about what becomes of a society that quietly eliminates fetally-detected maladies because of placing a high value upon the eugenics of infant perfectibility at birth. This is despite the fact that the people of Denmark, as a whole, embrace progressive policies of diversity, inclusion, and the protection of persons with physical and mental disabilities.

This means that parents choosing to receive their newly born children into the world, irrespective of what *in utero* genetic testing may reveal, subject themselves to the criticism of others who believe that evidence of potentially severe congenital defects warrants abortion. Moreover, those who elect abortion based upon the results of genetic testing may live with a sense of unease and shame in a nation that is one of the best at providing resources for persons with disabilities, and not least for those Down syndrome persons who can learn to read, write, work, and have a meaningful life. The state of Denmark provides them with healthcare, education, and "even money for the special shoes that fit their wider, more flexible feet."[45]

The author leaves us with the thought that possibly the time will come when we don't merely seek to screen out conditions that prevent individuals from being "normal," such as the extra chromosome-21 associated with Down syndrome, but instead we will see "all the anomalies that are compatible with life . . . actually expand our understanding of normal."[46]

Since being diagnosed with Parkinson's disease nearly four years ago, my symptoms have slowly progressed, such that I am reminded

---

[45]   "The Last Children of Down Syndrome," 44.
[46]   "The Last Children of Down Syndrome," 53.

many times a day that my body is not nearly so normal as it was. And while I'm uncomfortable with this fact, the not-so-subtle message I sometimes receive is this: "Whatever you do, don't allow Parkinson's disease to define you!" I hear this from both those who have the disease and those who have no idea what it is like for their bodies not to perform in response to what their brains tell them to do.

To say to people that they should not be defined by their disability is to say that their disability should remain as invisible as socially possible and acceptable, whatever that means. Accordingly, do we ever tell our children not to allow their successes to define them? Perhaps in many cases we should. But we usually pour time, energy, and resources into making sure their successes actually define them!

David Brooks, a New York Times columnist, notes the difference between "résumé virtues" and "eulogy virtues," the former being those that mark the skills and successes that people bring to the marketplace. On the other hand, "eulogy virtues" present a person's relationships as "bold, loving, [and] dependable."[47] When a society emphasizes "résumé virtues" over "eulogy virtues," those of us within that society tend to keep our failures and weaknesses, including our disabilities, hidden from the world and too often also from ourselves.

Possibly genetic testing will one day present parents with a choice of whether to abort or to give birth to the child, based upon whether test results reveal a genetic predisposition to Parkinson's. What then? We already know that where a familial history of Parkinson's is present there is greater likelihood that the disease will appear earlier in life than for those for whom Parkinson's is environmentally related.

What are the moral implications and consequences of undergoing abortion to prevent diseases that have an unpredictable onset

---

[47]   David Brooks, TED Talk, March 2014, https://www.ted.com/talks/david_brooks_should_you_live_for_your_resume_or_your_eulogy/.

and outcome, as well as indeterminable degrees of severity and suffering? Is the end-point of genetic medicine to be a state of perfectibility in which suffering is eliminated altogether? Whose suffering are we most of all talking about?

I think of my own life. What if my parents had known prior to my birth that the odds of my contracting Parkinson's were 90 percent by middle age, which as of four years ago happened to be 100 percent? If somehow, I could have said to them prenatally that I would much prefer to take my chances than to have no chances to take, am I not better off to be alive at this very moment and writing about my Parkinson's disease rather than to have missed fifty-six extraordinary years of life, even with all the suffering entailed? I put that question to you to ask of yourself.

I recently heard a physician friend describe a situation in which he promised an ailing patient's partner that he could "fix" her husband for her (we won't ask how), only to realize that the fix that was most needed had nothing to do with his body but everything to do with their social, emotional, and relational problems. The trouble is that we humans have ways of "fixing" things that often make things interminably worse than they were before the fix.

Consider then that God who raised Jesus from the dead does not seek to remove our suffering from us but rather to join our suffering by paradoxically entering into it with us—to the extent that God-in-Christ becomes humanly dismantled by the power of death which in Jesus's case was a violent death. Does knowing this, and believing this, place the entire discussion about genetic testing in a new light?

In his third memoir, entitled *No Time Like the Future*, which is about his own experience with Parkinson's, Michael J. Fox makes clear that he has indeed allowed the disease to define him. In response to his decision to pursue his acting career again after having abandoned it due to his illness, he wrote, "I began thinking more broadly about what possibilities my future could hold. Suddenly I was open for business again. Instead of allowing my idiopathy to deter me from employment, I created a new blueprint for myself: how to be a working actor with a disability. I'd co-opt the disease, get PD to do a little acting of its own, and bring my Parkinson's into the family business."[48]

Somehow, it is true that the revelation of God's weakness in the weakness of Jesus at Golgotha accentuates the reality of God's strength on Resurrection Day. When Saint Paul had had just about all he could take of the "thorn" in his flesh that continued to torment him, he looked at it this way: "Three times I appealed to the Lord about this, that it would leave me, but he said to me, 'My grace is sufficient for you, for my power is made perfect in weakness.' So, I will boast all the more gladly of my weaknesses, so that the power of Christ may dwell in me. Therefore I am content with weaknesses, insults, hardships, persecutions, and calamities for the sake of Christ; for whenever I am weak, then I am strong" (2 Cor 12:8–10).

So, let me ask you what I've asked myself more than once. By your weakness are you made strong? Is God's grace sufficient for all of your suffering?

The answer for me, time and again, is yes. The greater my weakness, the stronger my faith. The greater my weakness, the more Christ is revealed. The greater my weakness, the more I lean upon the only One who can ever save me anyway. And the sooner I accept my weakness, the closer I am to the contentment that Paul had learned but which is so evasive when we are focused only on our résumés.

---

48   Michael J. Fox, *No Time Like the Future: An Optimist Considers Mortality* (New York: Flatiron Books, 2020), 25–26.

PART SEVEN

LOOKING BEYOND
A CHURCH DISMANTLED TO
A KINGDOM RESTORED

CHAPTER THIRTY-FOUR

From Babylon to Jerusalem and from Captivity to Home!

May 2020

Thirty years ago during a deep personal crisis, I heard Wayne Watson's song entitled "Home Free." I listened to it and sang it over and over again. The chorus goes like this.

> Home free, eventually
> At the ultimate healing
> We will be home free
> Home free, oh, I've got a feeling
> At the ultimate healing
> We will be home free[49]

From the time we are born, we live in search of home. As wonderful as this world is, it can also be cruel, crippling, and unforgiving. Eventually we all wake up to this sobering fact.

The biblical story is one in which God's people repeatedly set forth upon a journey toward home, beginning from the time when God summoned Abraham and his wife Sarah to move out from Ur of the Chaldeans and on toward their new home in the land of Canaan.

Three generations later, Abraham's great-great-grandsons sold their brother Joseph, the son of Jacob whose name was also Israel, to

---

49   Wayne Watson, "Home Free," lyrics, https://genius.com/Wayne-watson-home-free-lyrics/. With permission.

the Ishmaelites who carried Joseph off into slavery in Egypt. It was there that the Israelites, as they were known, fell out of favor with the Pharoah who continued to enslave them. But God eventually delivered his people from their oppression by calling upon Moses to lead them across the Red Sea and through forty years of wandering in the wilderness until they reached the border of their new home in the Promised Land. It was from there that Joshua, son of Nun, a forerunner of Jesus, led the Israelites across the Jordan River where they settled into that very land that was to be flowing with milk and honey, until generations upon generations later their faithlessness toward God led them into exile yet again in a new home called Babylonia.

Simply put, our earthly home cannot remain our home forever. Being displaced and dispersed among a people who were their national if not mortal enemies made for a tough adjustment for the Israelites. Yet the prophet Jeremiah told them that they must settle down there and have children and build houses and be messengers of God's peace and prosperity to their new neighbors, seeking the welfare of the city. And then in due time the day would come, as God promised them, when they could go back to their old haunts in Jerusalem.

True to God's word, seventy years later, that day came when the Israelites were permitted to return to the holy city to rebuild its holy temple and once again call it home. And while those with long memories chose to do so, others decided to remain in Babylon where they had created comfortable lives for themselves. They had no interest in taking a chance on a home about which they had no direct knowledge or any compelling reason to return to. And so when the time came to decide, they turned back to their familiar digs in Babylon.

You could say that there were two "tribes" originally from the same "church"—one that headed back to its prior home which lay among the ruins of Mount Zion, and the other that was satisfied to stay in its Babylonian home among foreigners, where they and their families had been forced to live in exile.

But I have some questions: What if we present-day Christians are actually exiles ourselves? What if God is calling us to reside in a new "home" that is different from the one we've been living in? What if, after a figurative "70 years" since the dawn of the Enlightenment, God is releasing us from bondage to its chains? Or, to state the matter within a more recent frame of reference, what if the season of upward mobility that has defined the Baby Boomers has now come to an end?

Sociologists typically point to the year 1950 as a moment of particular significance in North America. As GIs returned from the Second World War, many social and cultural shifts began to take place, shaping the next seventy years that we are now looking back upon. Such as: rapid growth in higher education, increased middle-class affluence, widespread usage of the birth control pill for recreational sex, geographic mobility, rising divorce rates, burgeoning mass media promotion of pop culture, declines in church attendance, social movements challenging the status quo of societal institutions and authorities, and much more.

When writing *Road Signs for the Journey* nearly fifteen years ago, I cited such changes as reasons for the diminishment of church membership in the United States, concurrent with the general increase of secularization. As we became more educated, we became more "rationalized," if not per-se more rational, with respect to commonly held beliefs and social structures. As we became more geographically mobile, we became more individualistically focused and less accountable to the mutuality of community life. Some of us, though by no means all, accumulated more wealth for ourselves and greater reliance upon the coffers of aggregated corporate powers, thereby gaining a false sense of security and control over our destiny.

All of this meant that we became increasingly assimilated into a widely shared ecclesiastical milieu that saw little difference between the gospel of Jesus Christ and the smog of the "American Dream" wrapped around the churches. Before long we became perfectly comfortable captives of the so-called "good life."

For an entire century, sociologists had predicted the advent of this modern form of captivity, beginning with the German sociologist Max Weber writing in the early 1900s.[50] Weber predicted that the "rational" structures of the modern world—focused as they were on efficiency, predictability, control, and counting things—would lead to the loss of mystery and human creativity. Human beings, Weber said, would become prisoners within the "iron cage" of reason. He predicted that modernity would fall into a state of "mechanized petrification."

The solution, according to Weber, will be the timely rise of charismatic prophets who point to the captivity of persons who live inside of this "iron cage," as well as the rediscovery of those ancient ideals that can free them from their social and cultural imprisonment. In other words, prophets tell some hard truths that people profoundly, perhaps fatally, have forgotten.

By the 1950s, a new group of sociologists in Germany, called the "critical theorists,"[51] picked up Weber's warning about modernity and how it had captured just about everyone who had adopted its ways. Now some seventy years ago, these theorists were already critical of the new sexual freedoms and their consequences, and warned of the limitations of science, of consumer culture and its commodification of just about everything, and of the loss of personal creativity. They recognized that what had appeared to be a newly found freedom was actually a newly found bondage.

---

[50]   See footnote 6 in chapter 4.
[51]   See "The Frankfurt School and Critical Theory," *Internet Encyclopedia of Philosophy*. https://iep.utm.edu/frankfur/.

While shouts of religious "revival, revival, revival" have echoed here and there since the 1950s, perhaps what we have really needed is what we've got now, which is a broad displacement and dismantling that have the potential to dislodge the churches from enslavement to the idols of their cultural and political captivity. For the religious "center" of society is not "centered," if ever it was, in the precepts and powers of the liberating God who is revealed in the books of the Hebrew and Christian scriptures.

This present crisis within "church land," as the pews empty out and the doors of many houses of worship permanently close, may indeed be our summons to return "home," just as the Jerusalemites of Jeremiah's time returned to their home on "Mount Zion." "But 'Mount Zion,'" I hear some of you say, "can't be our home, for it is utterly devastated and fallen into ruin. We are far more comfortable staying right here where we are, slaves though we be, in our post-modern Babylonia with its capitol situated not on Mount Zion but in Washington, DC."

Yet, what if? What if, trapped as we are in that "iron cage," we listen now—not to our own predilections, but instead to the voice of the New Testament "prophet" Saint Paul? For, as he said long ago, "we look not at what can be seen but at what cannot be seen; for what can be seen is temporary, but what cannot be seen is eternal" (2 Cor 4:18).

Simply put, our earthly home cannot remain our home forever. Neither can our beloved bricks-and-mortar "church home." Yet since God is in the midst of us, then "home" is where God is, even if for a time this side of the New Jerusalem we live in exile.

CHAPTER THIRTY-FIVE

The Temple as Idol and the Church in Fast Pursuit

February 2021

In *Road Signs for the Journey*, I relied upon the prophetic words of Jeremiah to guide my understanding of the present situation of the American church.

One of the things that intrigued me about the sixth century B.C. Israelites was that their exile in Babylon, which coincided with the destruction of the Jerusalem temple, was directly tied to the fact that the temple had replaced God as the Israelites' locus of worship. God and God's Torah—God's teachings—had become incidental and largely irrelevant. The temple had become the idol of Israel's affection.

As is true of many American churches, you could say that the Jerusalem temple's order of worship was fixed, its seating (rather, its standing) arrangement was predictable, and the poor and marginalized remained on the edges. Predictable, comfortable, and secure were the bywords. Yahweh-God had become little more than a lingering afterthought.

Therefore, God took it upon himself to direct the Babylonians to enter and seize the city of Jerusalem, to take the people of Judah captive, and in the process destroy the temple. The point of it all was clear enough. To folks like Jeremiah, who had eyes and ears with which to see and hear what was going on beneath and above the surface, God was not going to allow a massive walled-in structure of stone and timber to remain an idolatrous substitute for the Holy One.

The temple was not to be a marketplace for commercial money changers to take advantage of the people who came to make their obligatory offerings. As Isaiah declared (Isa 56:7c), and as Jesus later repeated in the words of Jeremiah (Jer 7:11), "'My house shall be called a house of prayer'; but you are making it a den of robbers" (Matt 21:13).

Walling-out the alien, the foreigner, and anyone else who sought the shalom of God's kingdom, among other grievous collective iniquities, was not acceptable to God. For that reason, and for any persons who required a judicial explanation in order to understand just what God was up to within the temple-city of Jerusalem, God declared his "summary judgment" through the words of the prophet Jeremiah. Then God proceeded immediately to impose his "verdict" in the form of a sweeping demolition of the temple.

> Do not trust in these deceptive words: "This is the temple of the Lord, the temple of the Lord, the temple of the Lord." . . . Here you are, trusting in deceptive words to no avail. Will you steal, murder, commit adultery, swear falsely, make offerings to Baal, and go after other gods that you have not known, and then come and stand before me in this house, which is called by my name, and say, "We are safe!"—only to go on doing all these abominations? (Jer 7:4–10).

Of course, God's people deeply resented Jeremiah's prophetic words. But what the people failed to understand was that God's prophet was a "social analyst,"[52] a "history-maker," and a

---

[52] Walter Brueggemann, *Like Fire in the Bones: Listening for the Prophetic Word in Jeremiah* (Minneapolis: Fortress Press, 2006), 194.

"timekeeper."[53] He was following Yahweh's GPS, as it were, pin-pointed at the temple, indicating that God knew where his people were and what they'd been up to, and that he was going to demolish the stronghold of their disobedience.

As is so often the case with God's prophets, Jeremiah gained little respect and certainly no adherents. Is it inconceivable that this is also true of such prophets today? From my analysis of the situation of the American churches fifteen years ago, here is what I wagered to say about it.

Who can blame God's people for their resistance to Jeremiah's message, that all they held sacred was going to be destroyed? Who of us is willing to accept the disruption and death of those things we hold most dear—our religious practices, our religious identity, and the church buildings we cherish? This difficulty is painfully clear when congregations shrink to just a few faithful attendees. Efforts to revitalize such congregations are usually unsuccessful unless those who remain are willing to acknowledge the death of what they knew and allow God's Spirit to create a new future for them. . . .[54]

It seems especially difficult for adults and long-time church members to accept change and disruption in our churches. For this reason, the innovations and ideas of youth in the church are resisted. Too often young people hear, "But we've never done it that way before" or "we don't have the money for that" or "you didn't ask for permission." For many of us, history—rather than Scripture, the Spirit, or objective reality—shapes our decisions about what to accept or reject. Perhaps this is

[53]   Abraham Heschel's metaphors "timekeeper" and "history-maker" referenced by Elmer Martins, *Jeremiah, Believers Church Bible Commentary Series* (Scottdale, PA: Herald Press, 1986), 26–27.
[54]   *Road Signs for the Journey*, 136.

why Jesus said that it is the children, not the wise and learned, who will see the kingdom.[55]

Perhaps it's only the children passing by who notice and don't hesitate to say that the church has been reduced to skeletons buried in its graveyard, beneath tombstones that commemorate the dead.

For now, at least . . . until the coming Day of Resurrection.

---

[55] *Road Signs for the Journey*, 138.

CHAPTER THIRTY-SIX

Can the Church's and the Kingdom's Maps Converge?

February 2021

I once referenced the differences I see between established church people and my college-age students in terms of their capacity or desire to adapt their cultural maps to the realities of the Covid pandemic, as well as to what the pandemic reveals about the current social and political polarization.

Church people have seemed to me to be relatively frozen in their attitude, primarily saying, "Let's get back to normal" and "we have to re-open the church." In fact, it was hearing such responses among local church leaders in my community that prompted me to write that weekly email to my congregation in May 2020, which led to a year-long podcast entitled "A Church Dismantled—A Kingdom Restored." I had no idea then, and am surprised still, that my observations would resonate with so many people. This has given me some comfort in knowing that I'm not alone in the struggle about what to do during this precarious time.

My initial reaction was based in part on my resistance to the idea that the church is only a gathering of people existing in a particular cultural space and time, rather than, eternally speaking, a gathering of saints transcending space and time and place and culture. For it is the forces of modernity that have coopted us into believing that the church is confined by the cultural particularities of the present moment rather than commissioned to be a model of the world-transforming values of the kingdom of God.

So, just because a public stampede would return us to pre-pandemic societal and institutional norms and ways of life doesn't mean that the church should follow all of the horses charging into the corral. My concern has been that in the rush to regather between the walls and below the ceiling of the sanctuary, we may miss what the Spirit is calling us to be and do now, by way of realigning the cultural captivities of the church to the countercultural claims of God's kingdom.

What Jesus was up to in the Sermon on the Mount was to assert what my friend Don Kraybill so aptly called "The Upside-Down Kingdom."[56] For the kingdom of God that Jesus announced was not only turned upside down with respect to the Roman and Panhellenic culture of his day, but also with respect to his own Jewish culture. Jesus began his ministry with these words: "Repent, for the kingdom of heaven has come near" (Matt 4:17). Yes—repent—for as the Gospel of Mark reiterates, "The time is fulfilled" (Mark 1:15), meaning now is always the time to turn around and reverse course in response to the countercultural claims of the God's kingdom.

Witness this countercultural claim upon us from Jesus:

> "You know that among the Gentiles those whom they recognize as their rulers lord it over them, and their great ones are tyrants over them. But it is not so among you; but whoever wishes to become great among you must be your servant, and whoever wishes to be first among you must be slave of all. For the Son of Man came not to be served but to serve. . . ." (Mark 10:42–45a)

---

[56]   Donald B. Kraybill, *The Upside-Down Kingdom*, Anniversary Edition (Harrisonburg, VA: Herald Press, 2018 [1978]).

Yet another countercultural claim upon us from Jesus:

"It is easier for a camel to go through the eye of a needle than for someone who is rich to enter the kingdom of God." (v. 25)

Still another:

"You have heard that it was said, 'You shall love your neighbor and hate your enemy.' But I say to you, Love your enemies and pray for those who persecute you, so that you may be children of your Father in heaven; for he makes his sun rise on the evil and on the good, and sends rain on the righteous and on the unrighteous. For if you love those who love you, what reward do you have? Do not even the tax collectors do the same?" (Matt 5:43–46)

And another:

"Do not store up for yourselves treasures on earth, where moth and rust consume and where thieves break in and steal; but store up for yourselves treasures in heaven, where neither moth nor rust consumes and where thieves do not break in and steal. For where your treasure is, there your heart will be also." (6:19–21)

So, consider that there are two "heart maps"—the church's and the kingdom of God's. Where do the two "heart maps" culturally overlap, and where are they culturally miles and miles apart? By what coordinates do we of the church get our bearings? According to which map when one of them conflicts with the other? It's a decision we make every day on both sides of the pandemic.

Jesus said: "No one can serve two masters; for a slave will either hate the one and love the other, or be devoted to the one and despise the other" (Matt 6:24).

So let's choose our master. Because, to the one or to the other we will be obedient.

P.S.—Is that a decision we make before returning to "church"? What about after?

CHAPTER THIRTY-SEVEN

The Church Got Its Limen—
Now Will It Make "Limenade"?

February 2021

In 2007 in *Road Signs for the Journey*, I discussed the gripping uncertainty that God's people of Jeremiah's day felt while being hauled off from their beloved city of Jerusalem to what for all ostensible purposes seemed like an ill-fated exile in Babylon. Their thoughts and emotions were stuck in an abysmal state of "limen," which is defined as that ambiguous and threatening threshold between an old reality and a new one that most of us would avoid at all costs.

If you've ever been there yourself, then you know. Worse than being told you've got cancer are the days of anxious waiting between lab tests and the moment your doctor discloses the diagnosis. Worrisome and helpless feelings roil about in your stomach as you pace the floor, toss and turn in bed, and spin all kinds of dreadful scenarios around in your head. When you're caught in the "limen," you desperately want to know exactly what's going on inside your body in order to regain equilibrium and a sense of predictability and control over your life.

As for timely prayers to God, God may seem not to care in the least about your predicament: "What the heck is going on here, Lord?" you ask seventy times seven and then some.

You are a Jerusalemite. You're strapped in your sandals. You're weary and thirsty from having trudged along the hard-beaten, sun-bitten path into the big city of the great King Nebuchadnezzar. You know absolutely nothing of the place, except for rumors floating in the air about those legendary hanging gardens embellishing the royal palace.

Looking around, a queasy feeling hits you in the abdomen. You suddenly realize that the "limen" is not only your current state of mind, but it is Babylon itself. It is that discombobulating space between home and no-home where you must settle. The psalmist captures the moment.

"If I forget you, O Jerusalem, let my right hand wither! Let my tongue cling to the roof of my mouth, if I do not remember you, if I do not set Jerusalem above my highest joy" (Ps 137:5–6).

Liminal space can test you from head-to-toe and all in-between. What you yearn to remember—no longer stares you in the face.

Missional scholars have argued for several decades that the North American church at this very moment is in just such liminal space. It is languishing between an age-old, long-lost Christendom and a few remaining gravesites in the church's cemetery, awaiting burial of the last vestiges of what was.

Back in 2007, I wrote:

> If the church in North America has any chance of renewal, its members are going to have to accept that much of what we called sacred and holy is now dead, or at least on life support. . . . If we do not come to terms with our present disruption and accept our liminal reality, death will also come to terms with us. But for many of us, it may seem easier to die in denial, clinging to what is dear but false, than to realistically confront our demise in the name of the One who has overcome death and hell.[57]

---

[57]   *Road Signs for the* Journey, 138–140.

"So Conrad," you ask, "what is the answer?"

In response, I raise another question: What are we doing within this liminal space?

My wife Heidi always told our son Jacob, as do many parents, to make lemons into lemonade. Take what you've got and make the most of it.

Okay. So, what do we do with the "limen"? Can we make "limenade"?

Given the current social and cultural situation in which we find ourselves, are we making the best of this opportunity, the best perhaps in recent generations, by asking God to reshape us into his "kingdom people"? In other words, what do we "set" as our "highest joy"?

Jeremiah had an instructive word for the Jerusalemites feeling hog-tied in Babylon. He said, in so many words, stay in the limen. Settle down. Plant gardens. Raise your kids. Become comfortable with the uncertainty of your liminality. Bring *shalom* to your neighbors, and in doing so, *shalom* will come back to you.

During this pandemic, I don't think that our hankering to re-gather for public worship, fighting over masks, or joining the throng that attacked the U.S. Capitol will in any way provide us with the *shalom* that defines God's reign in the here and now.

But what can provide that *shalom*, that "highest joy," is the *word from on high* that Jeremiah offered on behalf of God to the "remaining elders among the exiles, and to the priests, the prophets, and all the people, whom Nebuchadnezzar had taken into exile from Jerusalem to Babylon" (Jer 29:1):

"Seek the welfare of the city where I have sent you into exile, and pray to the Lord on its behalf, for in its welfare you will find your welfare" (v. 7).

Here's the thing: *God* is incarnate in Babylon. *God* is the one invisible reality who in his apparent absence is always present. *God* has the power to turn "limen" into "limenade."

Drink deeply then of this moment. Drink deeply of God's word from the Good Book. For surprisingly good things can come to fruition in the land of exile.

CHAPTER THIRTY-EIGHT

More on the Limen, Parkinson's, and that River Ahead
February 2021

I've been thinking a lot over the past year about this liminal time for the church. When I was engaged in missional work with congregations, we sought to help them consider the value of a liminal moment. Liminal, as we have said, is that time between times, between cancer tests and the results, between being a child and being an adult, between the beginning of Covid and whenever the end of Covid comes, between the beginning of our pilgrimage and . . . you name it.

We like to avoid liminal spaces because they are thresholds between a place called "No Return" and a place called "Welcome Here." And there's no way to know what it will be like when we get there.

I was diagnosed with Parkinson's disease on February 14th, four years ago, which began my liminal journey between the time before Parkinson's and the time when Parkinson's will have taken its full toll on my body. As I told my students, I was able to see the end of my life approaching much more clearly than before the diagnosis. Consequently, I have felt a renewed energy and gained a clarified focus. I have stood taller with respect to my values. I have cared less than ever about conforming to the expectations of others. I am significantly more confident about my own expectations, motivations, and purposes. Being "liminal" has reinvigorated me, made me more human, and brought integration to the disparate pieces of my life. It has turned me into more of a whole person.

Not everyone has appreciated this change in me. Some have preferred that I be one person in one setting and another person in another setting, as when I more easily slid between social roles and wore different masks in different spaces. But Parkinson's has caused me to take off the masks. Given the time I have left, I want to be as authentically human as God created me to be. And that means I've also taken off the mask I'd been wearing before God.

So, what happens to church people when they become *maskless* people? Ponder that question. But let me ask it more personally. What happens when you remove *your* mask?

Every year as February 14th approaches, I think of my liminal journey through the past four years. I am aware of my increased impatience with those who simply want life to be "normal," to be what it was, to go back to living as they formerly lived. During this pandemic, for many church people that translates into getting as quickly as possible back to church.

But I grieve. I grieve because we are missing a chance to take our masks off, to sit with God in our inauthenticity, and to say to God, as Augustine did, "The house of my soul is too narrow for thee to come in to me; let it be enlarged by thee. It is in ruins; do thou restore it. There is much about it which must offend thy eyes; I confess and know it."[58]

It just may be, friends, that this liminal time is the time of deliverance from the secrets behind which we have lived, and to embrace the freedom that Christ offers us.

In *Pilgrim's Progress*, John Bunyan writes a beautiful passage about the ending of life.

---

[58]   St. Augustine of Hippo, *Confessions*, Bk 1.6 in *Augustine: Confessions and Enchiridion*, Albert C. Outler, trans. & ed., Library of Christian Classics, Vol. VII (Philadelphia: Westminster Press, n.d.), 34.

This river has been a terror to many, yea, the thoughts of it have often frightened me. But now, methinks, I stand easy, my foot is fixed upon that, upon which the feet of the priests that bare the ark of the covenant stood, while Israel went over this Jordan. The waters indeed are to the palate bitter, and to the stomach cold; yet the thoughts of what I am going to, and of the conduct that waits for me on the other side, doth lie as a glowing coal at my heart.

I see myself now at the end of my journey, my toilsome days are ended. I am going now to see that head that was crowned with thorns, and that face that was spit upon for me.

I have formerly lived by hearsay and faith; but now I go where I shall live by sight, and shall be with him in whose company I delight myself.[59]

In the margins of my prayer book, surrounding those words of Pilgrim, I have written: *"With a Parkinson's disease diagnosis I have begun to think of this season of life as 'the long road home.' Father, help me to walk this road with courage and confidence and hope; in you the living God, who will meet me at the River and take me into your eternal presence."*

Folks, every season is one in which we gain the ground with which to greet God face-to face. Since Pilgrim's story is our story, and until the time when our yet-to-be-seen future becomes our final destination, no season of life, liminal or not, need have been wasted.

---

59   Paul Bunyan, *The Pilgrim's Progress and Grace Abounding to the Chief of Sinners*, ed. John F. Thornton and Susan B. Varenne (New York: Random House, 2004), Kindle, 269.

CHAPTER THIRTY-NINE

Will I Ever Stop Talking About a Church Dismantled?
March 2021

A question has arisen from different corners and various people whose perspectives I respect, and the question goes like this: "Conrad, when will you move on from your focus on the subject of a church dismantled?"

There are many ways to hear and respond to this question, with just as many guesses as to what lies behind it. Perhaps the question reflects insecurity about changing institutional life and a desire to preserve the status quo. Or possibly it represents the anxieties of the leaders of dismantled churches whose living wage is sustained by their employment. Then, too, the question may pose understandable concern that my words about dismantling are in themselves tools of dismantling.

In my first stint of ministry, I received a similar question: "Conrad, will you ever preach anything other than about suffering?" I think that folks had begun to think I was a one-sermon preacher. Perhaps they were correct.

To answer in a broad sense, my response is twofold. To the first question, I say: when the church is eventually restored from its dismantled state. To the second: when there is no more suffering that needs to be addressed.

Comparable questions might be asked about a host of other related concerns, such as, how to respond to the temporal "powers" and "principalities," to the "rulers of the darkness of this world," and to the "spiritual wickedness in high places" (Eph 6:12, KJV).

Also, there are questions that faithful saints in faithful congregations press upon their faithful pastors to answer:

Why do you keep talking about racial injustices, since slavery in the United States has been a thing of the past for one hundred fifty years?

Why do you apparently dislike police officers, for where would our society be without the criminal justice system?

Why do you keep harping about right-wing evangelicalism and its embrace of White-supremacist nationalism and Trumpism?

Again, my response is twofold: when justice flows forth like a river to all people, and when the lion lies down with the lamb as God's people at last recognize that Christ alone is King over all earthly powers, including the churches.

That being said, the excavation of God's highway of righteousness within the wilderness of human affairs will not cease within the duration of human history. That's because in my lifetime and yours, the mountains of injustice will not be finally removed as obstacles to God's freedom. Neither will the valleys of human sin and sickness be raised up to heights where suffering forever ceases. Nor will the rough and crooked places of human bondage be straightened out into smooth plains where the oppressed are set free to walk without hindrance. For none of these divine reconstructions will be completed until God greets everyone on the other side of the River in the New Jerusalem.

This means that on this side of the Jordan where the baptismal waters flow, the church again and again will be called upon to bear witness to God's acts of justice, mercy, and love until that time beyond time when God's kingdom comes in full measure on earth as it is in heaven.

In the meantime, the kingdoms of this world will rise and fall, subject to the workings of God's righteous indignation accompanied by the deeds of God's judgment. Likewise, God's people will learn the wisdom of God's timing for tearing things down and building them up, and God's witnesses will give testimony to the hope that stems from the good news of God's grace and forgiveness.

We have recalled the days of the prophets Isaiah and Jeremiah, during which God dismantled the institutions of God's servant people, Israel. Not unlike ours, those were days and nights laden with grief and lamentation.

God said to Isaiah, "Go and say to this people: 'Keep listening, but do not comprehend; keep looking, but do not understand.' Make the mind of this people dull, and stop their ears, and shut their eyes, so that they may not look with their eyes, and listen with their ears, and comprehend with their minds, and turn and be healed" (Isa 6:9–10).

Isaiah then questioned God, as do we all: "How long, O Lord?" (v. 6:11a). For Isaiah knew that a prophet's word seldom gains acceptance.

God answered Isaiah: "'Until cities lie waste without inhabitant, and houses without people, and the land is utterly desolate; until the Lord sends everyone far away, and vast is the emptiness in the midst of the land. Even if a tenth part remain in it, it will be burned again, like a terebinth or an oak whose stump remains standing when it is felled.' The holy seed is its stump" (vv. 11b–13).

It is true then, isn't it, that God's ways remain inscrutable. Walter Brueggemann draws a conclusion for us to ponder in prayer:

> The prophet brings to public expression the dread of end-
> ings, the collapse of our self-madeness, the barriers and pecking
> orders that secure us at each other's expense, and the fearful

practice of eating off the table of a hungry brother or sister. . . . I believe that the proper idiom for the prophet in cutting through the royal numbness and denial is the language of grief, the rhetoric that engages the community in mourning for a funeral they do not want to admit. It is indeed their own funeral.[60]

Yet—it is also true that, beyond the cries of our communal grief, the prophet Isaiah offers God's promise of new life for the people: *"The holy seed is its stump,"* he said.

What then does the prophet's word mean for us in the time of our own dismantling?

It means that as followers of Jesus Christ we lean upon the assurances of the living Lord who speaks to us through the vision of the apostle John in the book of Revelation.

"See, the home of God is among mortals. He will dwell with them as their God; they will be his peoples, and God himself will be with them; he will wipe away every tear from their eyes. Death will be no more; mourning and crying and pain will be no more. . . . See, I am making all things new" (Rev 21:3–5a).

It is in this steadfast faith as disciples of Jesus that you and I live and die.

"If any want to become my followers, let them deny themselves and take up their cross and follow me. For those who want to save their life will lose it, and those who lose their life for my sake, and for the sake of the gospel, will save it" (Mark 8:34–35).

Ω

---

[60] *The Prophetic Imagination*, 50–51.